In Search of the Peak Experience?

Meditation has many purposes—spiritual growth, healing, past-life awareness, balance, mental clarity, and relaxation are just a few. *Meditation as Spiritual Practice* is a guidebook for inner evolution as well as for expanding consciousness into other realms.

As you learn to align your energy with seasonal, lunar, and planetary energies through meditation, you will experience states of expanded awareness. What we now call "altered states" and "peak experiences" will become the normal consciousness of the future.

Most persons think of peak experiences as something spontaneous which may happen, at best, only a few times in life. These experiences are a hallmark of spiritual development, and occur when you touch energy of a higher voltage than you are used to. This releases information in the form of visions or a sense of knowing, and initiates transcendental states that far surpass everyday existence.

This book is the complete guide for those who wish to claim higher vibrations and expanded awareness for their lives today.

About the Author

Genevieve Lewis Paulson is president of Dimensions of Evolvement, Inc., a nonprofit growth center located on 190 acres of the Ozark Mountains in Arkansas, a center of psychic, personal, and spiritual learning, accrediting students in the study of Kundalini energy development.

Not your typical New Ager, Genevieve is steeped in Western Christian tradition, and once served as administrator of a United Methodist Church. With the onset of a fierce Kundalini upsurge in 1968, she began her profound energy arousal, sought accreditation as a group leader in the fields of sensitvity training and conflict management—still under the purview of the church—only later discovering the ancient literature which described the Kundalini awakening she had been undergoing. Where her new experiences might have led her to abandon Western religious beliefs, she instead found a method to meld two varieties of truth, creating a synthesis of two great traditions of belief.

Genevieve teaches many of the classes at the Dimensions of Evolvement Center and also presents workshops in other locations. Much of her spare time is spent in gardening and photography.

To Write to the Author

If you wish to contact the author or would like more information about this book, please write to the author in care of Llewellyn Worldwide and we will forward your request. Both the author and publisher appreciate hearing from you and learning of your enjoyment of this book and how it has helped you. Llewellyn Worldwide cannot guarantee that every letter written to the author can be answered, but all will be forwarded. Please write to:

Genevieve Lewis Paulson
℅ Llewellyn Worldwide
2143 Wooddale Drive, Dept. 0-7387-0851-5
Wooddale, MN 551225-2989, U.S.A.
Please enclose a self-addressed stamped envelope for reply,
or $1.00 to cover costs. If outside U.S.A., enclose
international postal reply coupon.

MEDITATION

as

SPIRITUAL PRACTICE

GENEVIEVE L. PAULSON

Llewellyn Publications
Woodbury, Minnesota

First Edition
Sixth printing, 2005

(Previously titled *Energy Focused Meditation and Meditation and Human Growth: A Practical Manual*, 1994; and previously titled *Energy-Focused Meditation: Body, Mind, Spirit*, 2000.)

Cover images by BrandXPictures and PhotoDisc
Cover design by Kevin R. Brown
Interior illustrations by Randy Asplund-Faith

Llewellyn is a registered trademark of Llewellyn Worldwide, Ltd.

Library of Congress Cataloging-in-Publication Data

(ISBN: 0-7387-0851-5, Pending)

Llewellyn Worldwide does not participate in, endorse, or have any authority or responsibility concerning private business transactions between our authors and the public.
    All mail addressed to the author is forwarded but the publisher cannot, unless specifically instructed by the author, give out an address or phone number.

Llewellyn Publications
A Division of Llewellyn Worldwide, Ltd.
2143 Wooddale Drive, Dept.0-7387-0851-5
Woodbury, MN 55125-2989, U.S.A.
www.llewellyn.com

Printed in the United States of America

Other Books by Genevieve Lewis Paulson

Reincarnation (with Stephen J. Paulson)

Kundalini and the Chakras

The Seven Bodies of Man in the Evolution of Consciousness

Quick Fixes

Prayer is an Altered State

Tests and Steps on the Spiritual Path

Appreciation

Special thanks to Ralph Thiel, who not only put the entire manuscript on computer, through many revisions, but helped with editing as well. A special thanks for his patience and steadfastness.

Thanks to Stephen J. Paulson and Anne Thiel for editing.

Thanks to Ruth Allen, David Bahn, Jo Bahn, and Helen McMahan for their combinations.

Thanks to Rober W. Skelly, Michael Archibald, and Anne Lindstrom for their helpful comments.

Dedicated To

My Grandchildren:

Wendy

Matthew

Daniel

Noel

Brian

Ariel

Jessica

Elijah

Hannah

Nathan

Step Grandchildren:

Jeffrey

Jenny

Great Grandchild:

Amber Lyn

Step Great Grandchildren:

Joseph

Jaclyn

TABLE OF CONTENTS

SECTION II — MANUAL FOR EVOLUTION
THROUGH MEDITATION

INDEX OF CHARTS

INDEX OF ILLUSTRATIONS

FOREWORD

The energies of evolution slowly and relentlessly push the mass of humanity toward enlightenment. However, there are always those persons who stand out from the masses and who are not content with the slower form of progress. These persons are the ones to whom this book is directed.

INTRODUCTION

Meditation is quite often thought of as something unique to the Eastern religious traditions, with a particular form or structure. It is, however, a practice open to all persons, with many forms and structures. It is definitely not the same for everyone.

For some persons, walking in nature, having a quiet time, being at worship or in prayer can bring meditative states, with as much accompanying gain in development as with more formal meditations. My mother taught me (brainwashed me??) that the act of washing dishes was centering and soothing. The movement of the hands through the warm water can have a meditative effect. Anything that you do that has the quality of centering and tuning into energies is an act of meditation. We do need to develop a meditative attitude in all areas of life.

Basic meditation is a state of being which brings stillness to a person. During this period information may come in, energies may be heightened, and calmness or synthesis may be achieved. (It is not something a person actively does, it is something a person allows to manifest.)

It is possible, however, to focus on areas in which a person would like to achieve results. This book suggests various ways in which a person can develop and expand meditative abilities.

Focusing on the physical body with meditation can improve circulation, lower blood pressure and heart rate, bring calmer outlooks or more patience, boost the immune system, and give a person more control over his or her body, especially in the areas of pain, alertness, and healing.

Focusing on the emotions brings peacefulness, greater depth in relationships, and helps build a better foundation for motivation and for the development of spirit.

Focusing on the mental state brings clarity, greater effectiveness, more creativity, and helps to develop conceptual abilities.

On the spiritual level, meditation can bring a person closer to God and open new ways of being, which are beyond anything the human self can imagine.

Many people are feeling pulled toward this greater way of being and want to find more viable ways of living which growth through meditation can bring. The desire for more openness to higher levels of consciousness, to find out what else is "out there" or "in there," is developing a new frontier. Meditation is the vehicle for such pioneering.

Individual responsibility is incredibly important. It is great to have teachers, but ultimately it is up to each person to explore and choose what works for him or her in this field. Learning as much as possible about meditation can help a person make more effective decisions for growth.

SECTION I

MANUAL FOR MEDITATION

1

PLANNING YOUR
MEDITATION PROGRAM

M editation is usually thought of as only applying to spiritual growth or to achieving altered states of consciousness. This puts limits on an activity which can greatly affect
all of life. It is helpful for the beginner to look at the various
types of meditation, and for the more advanced meditator to
periodically explore other possibilities. Following are a variety of reasons for meditating.

- Stress reduction

- Serenity

- Understanding

- Centering and bringing the self into clearer focus

- Greater attunement of destiny energies

- Creativity

- Healing

3

- Relaxation

- Time-out from everyday concerns

- Past life awareness

- Increasing evolutionary energy flow

- Raising consciousness

- Paranormal abilities

- Physical, emotional, mental, and spiritual awareness and development

- Awareness of other dimensions and aspects of life, including angelic beings and other nonphysical forms

- Joy of expanded awareness

- Mental clarity

You may have some purposes to add to this list or discover new ones as your meditation abilities develop.

Ways to Use This Book

There are various ways in which you can use this book to develop and enhance your meditation skills. Below are several possibilities.

- You may wish to choose some simpler goals to begin with, such as stress reduction, "time-out" from everyday concerns, or centering and bringing the self into clearer focus. As you read the meditations, choose those which most nearly meet your primary goals.

Practice them until you have achieved the desired effect. Then set new goals and use new meditations.

• You may wish to go through the book and practice each meditation in turn until you have achieved the mastery you wish.

• Find exercises which can help you bring greater balance and awareness to your life and practice those.

In time you may wish to add variations to the meditations or develop your own.

It is recommended that beginners start with shorter periods and simple meditations. This helps a person adjust to the energy and also to not be discouraged by expectations which arise from the difficulty of maintaining longer periods of meditation.

For many persons a short period (ten–fifteen minutes) of meditation practice brings the benefits they would like. For others several hours may be required to fulfill their meditation needs. However, the longer periods may release too much energy before the system can adjust, so beginners should use caution.

Alone or with Others

Some persons prefer meditating with others. This may be done by forming a group which is similar in its intent and goals to your own. This can be very helpful. The beginning sessions should be exploratory, in order to find out what works best for the group. Some groups share leadership; others do best with one main leader. If you do start your own group, keep it small in the beginning and don't be surprised if some drop out. There are usually others who wish to come in later. It sometimes takes time for a group to "jell," or really work together well.

When a group works well together it can be difficult if new persons want to join. Sometimes they fit in and other times they may try to change the direction of the group to fit their needs. It is best for a well-established group to have a rule whereby new persons visit two or three times before any final decision is made about joining.

If you do not wish to start your own group, explore the groups that are available in your area. You should visit several times to see if you want to be a more permanent member, even if they do not have such rules.

Sometimes already established groups may have very different religious or moral beliefs from yours. Try to discern some of this information ahead of time. Meditation should enhance each person's particular belief system and allow them to expand on it, rather than totally supplant it. The best approach is to explore it well and be aware of your options.

If you wish to meditate alone, and many persons do, you may find it helpful to put the meditations you wish to do on a tape so that you aren't constantly stopping the flow to see what comes next.

The main benefits of meditating alone are that you can take plenty of time and go as deeply into a particular meditation as you wish. You are also free to meditate when it is convenient for you and to not be limited to whenever the group meets.

The best arrangement may be to do some meditating alone and some with a group. The solitary method leaves you with no one but your journal to share your experiences. It can also help to hear what happens to others in their meditations, as we grow by learning from others. If you only meditate alone, you may begin to wonder if your responses are normal. Sharing in a group provides this benefit.

There is another reason for meditating with others. The energy of a group is so strong that most persons find their meditations are stronger and have more clarity in a group setting.

Whatever you decide to do about your meditation practice, continue to be open to new possibilities in this field. The benefits are enormous and enlightened growth is essential.

2

HELPS IN MEDITATION

Meditation is basically a spiritual practice. To be in meditation is to be in tune with the greater spiritual self, thus the entire practice is one consciously or unconsciously directed to development in spiritual ways. Therefore, it is best if you approach meditation in a positive, spiritual way. You may wish to ask for God's protection before beginning.

Don't be negative with your meditations. If you think you won't get any place with them, *you won't*. Also, do not expect great things to happen when you are beginning. Just the practice of being in a meditative state can be very beneficial. Let come what comes.

PREPARING THE BODY FOR MEDITATION

Intruding thoughts happen to all meditators, beginners and more advanced. Your mind has probably been waiting for such a chance as this to bring these thoughts to your conscious attention. Many people find it very helpful to have a pencil and paper with them when they meditate so they can make notes of these thoughts. That practice will clear the system and make it easier to meditate. Also, you may find that there are things you have forgotten to do or there is some way to see a situation in a new light. If this does not help, focusing on the center of each eyebrow can help calm the mind.

It is better in the beginning to meditate for short time periods. If you feel irritable or nervous after having meditated, you may be bringing too much of the spiritual energy into your body to handle easily. If this happens you should cut your meditation time down or eliminate it altogether until your system adjusts to the vibrations of the higher energy. It is like 220 energy in a 110 body. It can blow fuses—that is, make it difficult to function.

Stretch well before meditation in order to loosen your body. You should also stretch very thoroughly after meditation so that you realign your system.

It is best not to get into any kind of breathing exercises, except simple ones, when you are a beginner. Many breathing exercises are so powerful that they release incredible amounts of energy, which may cause illness, crabbiness, inability to function well in the everyday world, or may release disturbing psychic phenomena. To breathe peacefully and deeply is generally sufficient in the beginning. If you will do this, you will find that your body adjusts your breathing to what is appropriate for you at the time.

Where to Meditate

In the beginning, it's best to find a quiet place and have some routine with your meditation. It can be helpful to meditate in the same place and at the same time every day. This is the way to build up your own meditation vibrations, which can then enhance future meditations. However, this method can also cause a dependency on that time and that place. It is much better to be flexible so that you can meditate any time or any place you wish. You may find it helpful to have the structured meditation and still develop flexibility by meditating off and on during the day in other locations.

You may sit or lie down. I've found it preferable that beginners, especially, use a lying-down position (without the head raised) because then there is no problem about whether or not the back is straight. The back should always be straight so that energy will flow correctly. Westerners usually do not have strong back muscles and will lean one way or another. Improper posture can cause the blockage of energy flow, bringing pain in the back, neck, or head; or it may release negative emotions. Some persons prefer a pillow under the knees which is very acceptable. This relieves any back strain. Some people need several pillows. Neck support can be a tiny towel filling the space between the flat surface and the vertebrae so that it does not alter posture.

Meditation must be practiced. It is the same as learning to play the piano, to paint, or to create. Practice is necessary for improvement.

You may find that some of your meditations feel completed in minutes and others seem to need a much longer time. You may also find that some are very intense and others very fleeting. Do not be caught up in expecting a pattern, otherwise it may block you from receiving something very special which may arrive in an unexpected manner.

If you find that negative things happen during or after your meditations, such as being aware of negative entities, unpleasant thoughts, or feelings, you may find that you have not sufficiently calmed yourself or prepared yourself for meditation. Some persons like to dance as a way of releasing energy and others find that the feeling of floating lifts them to the higher, more spiritual level. Praying for protection and guidance is also helpful.

Sometimes in meditation you may see astrally. For instance, you may see psychic bugs which represent things that bug you, or you may see other negative forms. Ask yourself what is bugging you or what the negative forms represent. When you have understood them and worked with them, they usually disappear. They are only your emotional or thought forms projected into your vision.

Involuntary Movements

Occasionally in meditations, a person may experience twitching of muscles, jerking of the body, or energy releases, which feel like little lightning bolts. Don't be bothered by this. It is just a sign that your meditation has relaxed you enough so that body tensions are being released. Energy will flow better afterwards.

Sometimes in meditations, a level of relaxation is so deep that tensions in muscles will release, thus bringing to consciousness memories of past experiences or attitudes. Observe them and let them play out their scenes. They may have been locked in the muscles system for years or for centuries (past-life influences). This is a form of cleansing blocked energies.

Symbolic Meditation or Fantasy

Occasionally the above will happen in symbolic form. A very strong "fantasy" will take over. This is the same as the above experiences, only it is happening in symbolic form. It has become a part of your own mythology. Observe it and let it work its way to an end so that its drama is completed. It usually will have its own completion, so don't try to stop it unless it's happening at an unsafe time such as while driving a car, working with machines, or at any time you need to put your full attention into what you are doing. If this happens, tell it you will come back to it later. It will be in your system waiting. You will know its completion, because you will feel a release of energy. You will feel lighter and more together.

Look for meaning when the "fantasy" has been completed. *Do not analyze or pick it apart while it is going on, because you interrupt the flow.* Usually you can't make too much sense of it anyway and trying to analyze it can stop it or garble it further. When the "fantasy" has completed, then you can analyze or pick it apart all you want. It can be treated similarly to the dream state, of which it is a form. *Becoming* the persons and objects generally will give you an understanding of the message, even if you do not comprehend the source of the fantasy.

Many times meditation experiences are very similar to dreams, and much meaning can be gained by working with this type of meditation as you do with your dreams. If you have a particular form you use in interpreting your dreams, you may wish to use that with meditation-induced "fantasies."

If your meditation-induced fantasies will not come to a satisfactory conclusion, or leave you feeling distraught, please seek professional help. You may also wish to fill your entire system with the color of lavender. This color is great for healing.

Out-of-the-Body Experience

It is very possible for a person to have such a good meditation that the physical body becomes disconnected from the astral-, mental-, or soul-level bodies. This is a common by-product of meditation. If you feel dizzy, lightheaded, disconnected, or experience a rocking motion during or after meditation, you may have started the process of out-of-the-body travel. All meditations should end by stretching the physical body thoroughly. This helps to synchronize all bodies and bring you back to everyday consciousness.

Sometimes persons actually leave their body and may travel away from the room where the meditation was taking place. If so, just thinking of being back in the physical body will aid in the return. It is nothing to fear, but it is good to know what to do about it.

If a person is slightly disconnected during meditation, or from a dream state, they may be aware of sounds which are not near them. It is possible to hear sounds in another part of the building or even much further away when the astral body has disconnected. (See page 143 for more information.)

Phasing Out

Persons may go so far in their meditations that they cannot maintain consciousness on the higher or deeper levels. They sometimes will think that they have been sleeping (and sometimes they are), but usually they have not developed a memory and consciousness bridge from their everyday awareness to higher levels. As they develop they will be able to maintain awareness at higher levels.

On occasion a person will be aware during the meditation, but afterward not be able to retrieve any information or awareness from the experiences which may have appeared at the higher levels. To feel the information or experience it in the physical body *as it happens,* as well as on the higher levels, will help build a memory bridge.

You should be careful not to become phenomena-oriented, as this can divert you from achieving the ultimate in growth-enlightenment. It's best to learn from the things you see, hear, and otherwise experience, and then let them go.

Meditation should not be used as an escape from life. It should be used to enhance life and to expand into one's greater self.

3

BEGINNING THE PROCESS

If meditation is new to you, or you feel overwhelmed by it, you may wish to begin with very simple "warm-up" types of meditations. It is best if a person doesn't strive too hard or set their goals too high in the beginning, as it is easy to lose enthusiasm if results aren't felt right away. It is not that easy to "measure" results from meditation anyway, since each person is different, the situations under which they meditate are different, and goals and expectations are different as well. Each person can only decide for himself or herself if something is working.

When you start to feel restless, bored, or that the meditations do not have the "lift" they used to, then it would be a great time to add more difficult meditations to your daily practice, or at least to vary the ones you are doing. Some persons keep journals of the meditations they do and the results achieved. These are helpful to review, as they remind us of where we've been and what we've done.

STEPS IN MEDITATION

1. Choose your meditation (you may wish to put it on a tape or have someone guide you through it).

2. Concentrate on the focus of the meditation for a few moments (your energy will be active and outgoing).

3. Let go of the concentration and open to the receptive state—meditation. Be aware, do not judge what is going on as that can break the meditative state. (You can judge or pick it apart afterward.) If you find yourself very uncomfortable with the exercise, you may wish to stop it.

4. Sometimes a person will become so in tune with whatever is being meditated upon that a state of *contemplation* or oneness is reached. This seldom happens in the beginning.

5. Recall is very important after a meditation. Writing it down is usually best, or it may be shared with someone.

   By recalling the experience you develop greater awareness, develop a memory bridge to other dimensions, begin to develop your "spiritual" language, and also increase your growth from the exercise.

Warm-up Meditations

Those who exercise know a warm-up period enhances the exercise program and makes it easier on the body.

So, too, with meditation. With a warm-up period a person is more likely to "settle" into the meditation quickly and easily, and will also find that he or she will usually go deeper and get more benefit.

Below are some "warm-up" meditations. They may be done by themselves or followed by additional meditations.

1. This is a simple breathing exercise where the concentration is on the numbers, for the purpose of relaxing the system.

   Sit or lie quietly, breathe peacefully and deeply, and watch your exhalations. Count them up to four and then start over again: 1, 2, 3, 4 — 1, 2, 3, 4 — 1, 2, 3, 4. Do this until you feel your body is relaxed and integrated.

2. Listen to sounds. How many sounds can you hear at once? This exercise helps bring alertness as well as relaxation.

3. Sit or lie quietly. Begin with your feet and relax your body all the way to the top of your head. This is a great exercise for relaxation. You may not feel like working afterward, however.

4. Be aware of energy outside of your body for a few minutes. Then be aware of energy inside of your body. Do it slowly and alternate it four or five times. This is great before meditations, or just to tone your system.

5. Use breathing as a way to center. Be in a comfortable position, with your back straight. Let your breath be even, peaceful, and deep. Get into the rhythm of the breath and feel your body relax.

Basic Meditations

Following are some basic, easy meditations you may wish to practice before beginning the more structured ones in Chapter 4.

Music

Use meditation music as a background or focal point. Be either in a lying-down position, or comfortable, sitting position. Either way, make sure your back is straight, because energy travels through the spine and it needs to have free passage. Tune in to the music, be one with it. Let any thought or feelings just pass right on by. Don't get caught in them or have the feeling you have to push them away. Just be and let them be.

Colors

Be in a comfortable position, with your back straight. Fill yourself with the rainbow colors, one at a time. If you can't see them, just imagine they are spreading throughout your body. Energy follows imagination and it will work just as well. Start with red, follow with orange, then yellow, green, blue, purple, and end with radiant white. A total of ten minutes is plenty.

Sitting

Be in a comfortable position, with back straight. Loosen your shoulders, wrists, and ankles. Feel the rest of the body begin to relax. Just "be" for ten or fifteen minutes, with nothing to do or think.

Space

If you feel overwhelmed by others' energies and the rush of life, begin with the sitting or lying-down position. As you breathe, feel your chest open up and then let the rest of the body open up, giving you a feeling of plenty of space inside. Appreciate the space. Fill it with love, peace, or some other quality.

Nature*
by Jo Bahn

This helps bring oneness with nature through pictures. Select a photograph of a place in nature such as a waterfall, ocean, rock formation, meadow, mountain, desert, pond, or any other place that appeals to you. Seat yourself comfortably with the picture in front of you. Use the floor or table, whatever is appropriate for you. Fix your gaze on the

---

* Meditation printed with permission of Jo Bahn, Willowend, Jacksonville, FL.

picture and focus on the scene with its associated feelings, thoughts, and awarenesses. Simply look at the picture and fill yourself with the image until you are one with it. In the beginning do this exercise for five minutes. Gradually increase to ten or fifteen minutes. Change the picture occasionally to experience different aspects of nature.

Brain

Sit or lie quietly. Feel your brain gently expanding and quiet. Imagine your breath is going into it, bringing openness. After a few minutes, expand your energy to the space around your head. Be aware of that for a few minutes and then just be. As you stay quiet and open, new information may come in or you may just find that you are more relaxed. However, as you continue to practice this meditation, it will increase your intuitiveness and creativity. You will also find you comprehend information more easily (for more information on brains, see page 95).

4

MEDITATIONS TO BROADEN DEVELOPMENT

O ne of the greatest pitfalls of meditation is to continue doing the same one for years. Granted, it is great for relaxation and centering, but it tends to develop a person in only certain areas. This practice digs the same hole deeper. The broader, more expansive benefits which may come from meditation are not achieved. This chapter is designed to expand your capabilities, open you to new areas, and bring out greater benefits and possibilities of living for you.

We begin with the focused type of meditation. Since part of the purpose of meditation is to train a person to function in more viable ways, meditations with a "focus" or direction usually work best. The beginner, as well as the advanced student, will benefit because these meditations help broaden their experiences.

Also, without a focus the person may be more easily distracted or uneasy, thus blocking the development of the receptive meditative state.

Following are a variety of meditations with focuses that assist in overall development.

FOCUS ON SELF

The Physical Body

The physical body is very important in spiritual growth. A person can develop only as far as his or her physical body will allow. If the physical body stays dense, heavy, and full of blocks, the meditation energy will have a difficult time moving through the system. This creates aches, pains, crabbiness, and a general feeling of being a prisoner in your own body.

Using meditations to help develop the physical body greatly enhances growth. As our physical bodies become lighter, freer, and the cells more developed, we begin to see our bodies as our allies rather than our jailors.

Focusing on the body can include movement such as dance, stretching and physical exercises, as well as breathing exercises. It may be awareness of energy in the body, or the distribution of energy through the opening of chakras (energy vortices), and balancing of energies in the body. It may include sending healing throughout the body.

Breathing Meditation for Centering and Opening the Body

Be in a comfortable position. You may wish to start by lying down, with no pillow under your head, for the first time. It also may be done sitting or standing.

Take deep, peaceful breaths. Let them go all the way through your body. Feel the energy of the breath go into your feet and beyond them. Then add an awareness of the energy of the breath going all the way through your hands and beyond them. (In order to feel the energy going out, you may imagine it is the breath which goes all the way out.) After you have the energy going out the feet and hands then increase your awareness to include the energy of the breath going out the top of the head. Feel the energy field around you. After a few minutes of this breathing you may choose to rest in a relaxed state. You may then choose to follow this with another meditation, as it is a good preparation exercise.

Meditation for Stress Reduction

Begin by relaxing your toes, then the feet, ankles, and on up the body to the top of the head. Breathe into each area, feel new strength going into each cell. (Don't forget your arms.)

Close by having the feeling of floating for a few minutes. Visualizing light blue helps achieve the floating sensation. (This can lift you to higher levels where you experience "chills." That is great!)

Meditation for Mobilizing Stress

This is an excellent meditation when you have much to do and can't seem to get mobilized.

Lie down, be comfortable. Visualize things you wish to do and feel them in your body at the same time. Seeing and feeling are both important.

Imagine you are doing the task. Both see yourself and feel yourself doing it. What information comes through? Allow yourself to rethink what you are about to do and how you are planning to do it.

Generally this helps to get you on your feet and into action.

Meditation for Energy Balancing

Be aware of the energies on the right half of your body. Then be aware of the energies on the left half of your body. Do this several times until they feel balanced, and then feel the energy on the left and right sides together.

Feel energy in the front half of your body and then the back half of your body. Do this several times until you can feel them equal. Then do front and back together.

Be aware of the energies from the waist on up, and from the waist on down. Do this several times until they feel balanced, and then feel the energies in both the top half and bottom half of your body, and feel synchronized.

Meditation for Healing

Ask to feel healing energies in your body. Then be aware. Where does there seem to be energy movement in your body? Let it do its own thing for about five minutes in the beginning. Later you may work up to longer periods of time. Be careful. Do not do this for more than five minutes at a time until you are more used to the energy, as the healing energy can release much blocked negativity and start the cleansing process faster than is comfortable to handle. After the healing energies do their own thing for awhile, you may direct the healing to specific spots in your system for a few minutes more.

Meditation in Movement

One of the simplest, easiest, most excellent examples of meditation in movement is free-form dancing. Have music as a background and then let your body move as it wishes to the music. This is a wonderful way to release blocks and to free your energy. This exercise also does not need to be done for a long period of time. Whatever is comfortable for you is best. Remember, it is your system and your body that you are working with and you know best when to quit.

Emotional (Feeling) Body

It is very important to include the emotional, or feeling, level in some of your meditations. In many ways, this area needs relaxation and cleansing more than some of the others. Well-developed emotions are the basis for good development of spirit. Below are some meditations which may be used.

Our emotions are active all of the time. It can be very helpful to tune into them. It helps us to be more aware of our emotional directions and what we're doing about them.

Meditation of Rebelliousness

Everyone feels rebellious at one time or another. This exercise can help you to explore these energies and help you to make better use of them.

Be in a comfortable position with your back straight. Be aware of your belly area, around the navel and solar plexus. These are areas where these feelings quite often are stored. Be relaxed, open up and be aware. How would you like to be a rebel? Against what or against whom? Or would you like to rebel against yourself? Really get into these feelings, explore them. Where do they seem to be coming from in your body? Stay with them until you get the deeper meaning behind them. Then ask yourself what you have been gaining by having them. More independence? Pushing people away? More privacy? Release of energies? Getting even? Standing up for yourself? A chance to explore your own beliefs? Then, ask if there might be some easier, better way to accomplish the same things.

If meditation does not resolve the rebelliousness, then fill yourself with the color lavender, which aids in healing.

You may wish to substitute other feelings such as joy, anger, sulking, loneliness, etc.

Meditation for Gaining Inner Strength

Our inner strength (usually) falters on the emotional or feeling level first. This exercise can help you develop this area. Feel strength in your back, especially your spine. Then let that feeling spread to your entire body. Then let your heart be filled with love to balance the strength. How does that feel to you? It is possible to be very afraid of your own strength, your own power, when it is not balanced with love. Feel strength in your lower belly. Do you let yourself have "guts"?

Meditation for Cleansing and Relaxation

(You may wish to use a record or tape with the sounds of the ocean for this one.)

Imagine you are a beach. Your feet correspond to the part of the beach next to the water. Let the tide come in and wash you clean as it flows back out. Be into this feeling for a few minutes or as long as you wish. As the water washes the beach, think of the peace of God cleansing and calming you.

Meditation for Developing Feelings

Choose a feeling such as contentment, peace, patience, or joy of life, and feel it in your belly. Let the feeling spread throughout your body. Doing this meditation every day for a few minutes works wonders.

The Mental Body

Meditation on Thoughts

The mental area needs to be open and expanded—otherwise thinking will be narrow, prejudicial, or there may be blind spots in one's perceptions.

An open mind can be a joy as new ways of being, thinking, and acting are comprehended. Meditating is an excellent way to develop this area.

The thoughts may be ideas, spiritual texts or qualities, possible solutions for problems, or greater awareness. When you focus on a thought, concentrate on it for a few minutes. Really put your thinking abilities into it—whatever it is—whether it's an idea, problem, or something else. Concentrate for a few moments on your selection. Then be open and let the idea or problem give information back to you. Be aware. What thoughts come to your awareness? Information may also come through pictures or sound.

Meditation for Exercise on Ideas

Think of an idea that you have. Concentrate on it—you may even wish to write down what you know about it first. Then open your mind and be aware. What information comes back to you? Then ask it to expand. What other possibilities are there?

Meditation on Problem Solving

Concentrate on the problem. Be aware of as many aspects of the problem of which you know. Then put your attention above your head so you are open beyond your brain area. Open yourself to receiving. This is the point where illuminations come in—from fleeting thoughts to new insights, or, in some instances, an awareness of cosmic consciousness.

Meditation on Brain and Body Balancing

Lie down in a comfortable position. Relax and let loose of all tension, especially in the neck area.

Feel energy in the right side of the body. Then send that energy up the right side, cross over in the lower back of the head and up into the left brain. Really feel the connection for a few minutes.

Feel energy in the left side of the body. Then send that energy up the left side, through the lower back of the head and into the right brain. Really feel the connection for a few minutes.

Feel total balance all over the body and head. Breathe into the entire system and increase the energies through deep breathing. A few minutes is usually long enough.

This is an excellent preparation exercise for meditations in general and particularly for the following one.

Meditation on Brain Balance for Creativity

Breathe into the left brain; increase its energy and alertness by feeling that you are breathing into it for a few minutes. Then repeat doing the exercise with the right brain.

Balance both brains, feel the *corpus collosum* (bridge between the brains—hemispheres) as being open and functioning well.

Let the energy from the center of the brains come up and out the top of the head. Meditate on the space above your head and ask what creativity is waiting for you?

Meditation on Choosing a Path or Making a Choice

List the various choices you have, no matter how farfetched. Then meditate, taking each path or each choice in turn. Be aware of your thoughts and feelings. Take a good look at how each one evolves and what possibilities are there? This can give you more information so that you can make a better choice.

Meditation on Expanding Intelligence

Let energy go out of the top of the head and the bottom of the heels. Be balanced. Ask to know something you didn't know previously. Let your thoughts ramble. What information comes in? Don't rush this. Give the energy time to form the new thoughts.

The Spiritual Body

We all have a spiritual side to ourselves, which must be nourished and exercised in order for it to grow. Not all meditations are directed to this area and some care needs to be given to it as well. Below are some suggestions for development of this area.

Meditation on Spiritual Qualities

Choose a quality such as love, compassion, understanding, or joy, and then let yourself be filled with it. Where in your life do you express this quality? Where in your life should you do more with it?

Meditation of Spiritual Concepts

Think of what eternal life means to you. Think of it and be aware of it all over your body. Then let go and feel the concept of eternal life, and let it speak to you.

Meditation on Spiritual Texts

Choose a favorite text from the Bible or some other spiritual book. Feel it in your body—be one with it and open to new insights.

Choose a text that troubles you, or with which you don't agree. As you feel it in your body, what information comes to you?

Oneness With God

This is being and feeling one with God, your Creator, or whatever name you use for your conception of ultimate reality. Do not get hung up on terminology. Use whatever name or concept has meaning for you. This is a wonderful form of meditation or attunement with God. This exercise can help you understand your own sense of divinity, your connection with God, with the cosmos, and your destiny.

Be in a calm, peaceful, receptive attitude and feel the presence of God in and around you. Feel the presence surrounding you and filling you. Be open to any insights which you receive.

There will be more meditations for this in later chapters.

Meditation on Religious Symbols or Persons

The object can be a special flower, a religious symbol or object, or a picture of a religious or spiritual personage. Let yourself become one with the symbol, the object, or personage. Expand your energy and open to the power you feel coming into you.

Caution: Many persons like to meditate staring at a candle flame. I do not recommend it for beginners as it may develop a trance state. If you do not know what you are doing, it may open you to a lower astral level and leave you open to the influence of

White and Chromatic

Purple

Blue

Green

Yellow

Orange

Red

Earth Brown

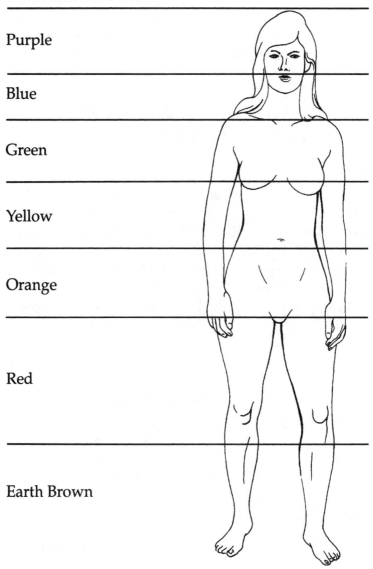

Figure 1

Chakras (energy vortices) located in a particular band will generally display the corresponding color. A highly developed chakra will contain the full spectrum.

negative energies or negative entities. The candle flame is listed in many books on meditations, but I recommend you begin with something else, unless you are with a trained teacher or you have reached a higher level of evolution.

SYNTHESIS OF OUR BODIES
FOCUS ON PLANES AND BODIES

Our cosmos is made up of seven great planes—physical, emotional (astral), mental, intuitional/compassionate, will/spirit, soul level, and divine level. In our beings we have "bodies" which can vibrate with these different planes.

The first three levels (bodies) relate to the personality. The remaining four (the intuitional/compassionate, the will/spirit, the soul, and the divine) relate to the spiritual or expanded levels. They deal with what are sometimes called "transcendent" levels; that is, they transcend the personality levels. Sometimes these four are all included in the spiritual level. However, as one develops it is better to work with them separately.

We function best when our bodies are balanced and all of them operating. In many persons one body is dominant. Generally, either the emotional or the mental is dominant.

Below is an exercise which helps to develop awareness of the bodies, thus helping to develop greater balance and effectiveness. Spending some time with each level helps to balance them.

Meditation of the House of the Seven Bodies

This exercise deals, in a symbolic way, with whether or not we "live" in our bodies (they relate to the planes mentioned above) and our attitudes toward them. Have paper and pencil handy to write down impressions.

Either lie down or sit comfortably, with eyes closed. Breathe peacefully and deeply for a few minutes, then visualize a house with seven rooms, one for each body.

First, enter the room for the physical. What does it look like? What colors are used? How is it decorated? Are you comfortable there? Does it looked lived in? Do not make any changes at this time, but write down your impressions and then continue through the rooms, always writing down your impressions.

After finishing the exercise, look at your notes. Which body seems to be lived in most? Which least? Where do you sense problems?

Repeat the exercise, this time changing the rooms in any way you would like. (You may feel "psychically tired" and wish to leave this part of the exercise until you have rested.)*

COLORS AND BODIES

Following is a meditation which helps awaken the areas (see figure 1) that relate to the different body levels. This also helps to bring balance in the system.

The chakras (energy vortices which aid in our development) are shown as they correspond to the various levels.

Meditation (see figure 1)

1. Begin with the feet. Feel their connection with Earth (you can do this even if you are in a high rise building, as the feet's vibration relates to Earth.) Fill them with a coppery brown. Ask for strength and awareness to come into the area from your feet to just below your knees.

---

* This exercise is based on one from the pamphlet, *The Seven Bodies of Man in the Evolution of Consciousness*, by Genevieve Lewis Paulson.

2. Fill the area from below your knees to the top of your pubic bone with a clear red. Feel the energy of security and purposefulness. Feel strength and awareness developing.

3. Fill the area from the top of the pubic bone to just below the navel with orange. This is the sexual area, and its energy also transmutes into power, action, and creativity. Feel strength and awareness developing in this area.

4. Fill the area from just below the navel to below the heart with a light yellow. As the yellow goes into this emotional area it can bring clarity. Feel strength and awareness develop in this area. Include your arms in this part.

5. Fill the area from below the heart to the base of the neck with a green color. Let the energy of living your life and embracing your visions fill this area. Let strength and awareness develop in this area.

6. Fill the area of the neck up to the bottom of the nose with blue. Feel the energy of speaking, eating, and interacting with others. Let strength and awareness develop in this area.

7. Fill the area below the nose to the top of the head with purple. Feel the energy of seeing and comprehending. Let strength and awareness develop in this area.

8. Fill the very top of your head with radiant white. Feel the energy of spirit lift you up. Feel strength and awareness develop here.

Close the exercise by being aware of yourself from your feet and hands to the top of your head. Also be aware of the force field of energy around you. Breathe peacefully and deeply while the new strength takes hold in your system and you find yourself much more aware of your entire body.

5

USING SENSES AS MEDITATION TOOLS

HEARING

You may hear sounds from inside you or outside of you. They can be repetitive, which helps to create a particular thought form. They can help alter your state of consciousness in a variety of ways. For sounds outside of the self; music, nature, bells, chimes, or any sound around you may be used. Sounds from inside can include; vocal prayers, speaking of litanies, singing chants, hymns or phrases used routinely.

Various forms of music can help give different vibrations in order to achieve other states of consciousness. There are many excellent meditation tapes and records available in New Age stores.

Meditation 1 — Sounds Outside

Be in a comfortable position. Listen to sounds around you. Focus on one at a time, becoming a part of the sound. Let pictures, thoughts, or feelings emerge. This can help to cleanse, center, and lift you up.

Meditation 2 — Sounds Inside

Be in a comfortable position. Listen to sounds inside yourself. Rather than hear them, you may feel their vibrations. Become one with them. What information comes to you? This exercise also is a form of cleansing, centering, and lifting of vibrations.

Meditation 3 — Tones

There are tapes available from various sources with repetitive tones which help in achieving various states of consciousness. You may purchase these or work to develop your own.

(Llewellyn Worldwide, Ltd. has some great "tone" tapes.)

Meditation 4 — Voice

From your memory, recapture a conversation you've had recently. How did your voice sound? Did it affect what you were trying to say?

Develop a habit of listening to your voice. Does it convey the meaning of your words or the essence of who you really are?

Meditation 5 — Music

Listen to different types of music. Which ones center you, help your creativity, inspire you, or create other vibrations which are helpful to you? The power of music to create change in the system is phenomenal.

Meditation 6 — Mantras or Repetition of Words

Following are some suggestions. You may wish to repeat them to yourself for three to five minutes and see what the effect is on your system. These should lift your consciousness and bring new levels of awareness.

Praise God
Thank God
Ohm (Sanskrit meaning everything and nothing)

Meditation 7 — Music and Chants

Gregorian chants have been used in the Roman Catholic Church for centuries. Listen to a record or tape of the chants. Let the sound fill your body and mind. Humming with them or singing with them can be very helpful. What awareness does it bring? Listen to those hymns or other religious songs which have special meaning to you. What awareness or feelings arise?

The Doxology has been used much in Christian tradition and may be said or sung as a chant.

Praise God, from whom all blessings flow;
Praise Him, all creatures here below;
Praise Him above, ye heavenly host;
Praise Father, Son, and Holy Ghost!

If you use chants with foreign words know what the words mean and pronounce them correctly so you do not change the meaning. The Gyuto monks have a video cassette available with which you may wish to chant.

Body Sounding

Relax, let go of control. Begin to breathe deeply and let sounds come into your breaths. Don't hold them back, let them emerge. You may exaggerate them if you wish. How many different sounds come from your system? Ah's, hums, groans, and giggles are some sounds which like to surface.

This is usually very refreshing and empowering. On occasion it may release deeper feelings which have been blocked. Observe them, feel them, and let them go. A little extra "sounding" may be needed to clear the system.

If something comes up that is too difficult to handle alone, do get some help from a counselor or therapist.

SIGHT

Our lives are greatly influenced by what we see—or allow ourselves to see. We have tendencies to block perceptions by tightening muscles around our eyes.

Meditation 1

Massage around your eyes, including your temples. Then look around you. Can you be more aware of what you see? How many colors can you see and receive vibrations from?

Meditation 2

Look at a picture—preferably one in your home. Become each part of the picture. Feel the energies in your body. What effect does it have on you?

Then feel the total picture in your body. What is the message here?

Meditation 3

Look in your closet. Feel what you see in your body. What effect does it have on you?

SMELL

You can help develop your awareness skills through the use of smell. Smell is very important in our lives. It tells us when something is not right to eat or be near. It lifts us up when the odors are beautiful and touch deeply into us. Perfumes, foods, and flowers all can raise our energies to more positive and higher vibrations if they are something which resonates with us. You can help develop your awareness skills by increasing your sense of smell.

Meditation 1

Be in a peaceful state and close your eyes. Massage the sides of your nose (nasal glands are located there). What do you smell around you? Does it bring you up or drag you down? How many smells can you identify? Which ones do you wish to change?

Meditation 2

Focus on a particular scent, whether from a flower, perfume, or some other source. Slowly and peacefully inhale the essence of the scent. Let its energies fill your body, bringing a feeling of expansion. Sit with it for awhile. What new awareness and experiences come to your attention?

TASTE

Most of our taste actually comes from the process of smelling. The only things we really taste are sweet, sour, bitters, and salt. These concepts also apply to experiences which happen to us in daily life. Following is a meditation to explore this.

Meditation

Imagine the taste of *sweetness* in your mouth. Do you need to bring more sweetness into your life in general? Or do you hide from sweetness, feeling that you don't deserve it?

Imagine a *sour* taste in your mouth. Do you like to flirt with sour? Love the taste of pickles? Enjoy the extra dimension sourness brings to your food. Is there sourness in your life you could appreciate more for its flavor?

Imagine a *bitter* taste in your mouth. Feel how it makes you more aware, heightens your senses. Is there something going on in your life now which relates to bitterness? How can it open your awareness so that you can make new choices?

Imagine the taste of *salt* in your mouth. Does it make you more aware of yourself? Do you feel sharper, as though you are more effective? Do you feel that more of your essence is expressed?

TOUCH

Touch is important for everyone, whether it is touching someone or being touched, feeling the sensation of the clothing which we wear or some other form of touching. The act of touching can bring greater awareness and aliveness in our systems. It is an important part of our senses and should be consciously practiced. Below are some suggestions:

- Touch all of the objects around you. Note how your body opens up.

- Massage your arms. Feel the skin's sensory apparatus awaken. You may wish to find a good lotion and massage your entire body. You may get massages from others, but when you do it yourself you are putting your own energies into your body and heightening your sense of self.

- Stroke a pet. They love it (most of them do, check it out first). Feel oneness with a species other than human. You may wish to do the same with a tree, rock, or plant.

- Touch different types of materials with your eyes closed. What thoughts and associations come to mind? What feelings come to your awareness?

- Hold your hands open and facing away from you. Breathe peacefully and deeply. What vibrations can you feel around you?

- Do the action in the previous paragraph outdoors and include a feeling of petting the air.

- Lift your hands up and let them be open. Ask that God fill them with love.

6

FOCUS ON EARTH
AND HEAVEN

ROCKS AND MINERALS

For centuries persons have used stones and minerals for various purposes including healing, heightened powers, protection, and consciousness raising. You may also find other ways to use them.

It is best to pick out specimens that really feel connected to you. Each one seems to have its own personality.

Below are several meditations to help you explore your relationship with the mineral kingdom.

Meditation 1

Choose a particular rock, turn it over in your hand and look at it. Then either keep it in your hand or place it on your body and close your eyes. Be in tune with the energies of the stone.

Meditation 2 — Rocks for the Seven Bodies

The rocks in this exercise are chosen for their energy, which corresponds with and expands particular vibratory rates or bodies which help make up our

	Chart 1		
	ROCKS AND BODIES		
Level	Body	Rock	Rock Description
1	Physical	Gold sheen obsidion	Black with orange markings
2	Emotional	Onyx	Pale yellow
3	Mental	Rose quartz	Pink, smooth
4	Intuitional/ compassionate	Barite	Brownish crystal
5	Will/Spirit	Magnetite	Blackish, magnetic
6	Soul Level	Smithsonite	Pink, gray, blue, green or lavender
7	Divine Level	Crystal	Clear or whitish

system. See Chart 1 above for brief descriptions of the rocks and the body to which they relate.

Expansion – As you use the rocks and meditate on the function of the body with which you are working, be aware of that area expanding, opening up. This is the first step—expansion, opening up.

Awareness – Because the body has expanded, you need to begin awareness. You may ask the body what it needs from you, or you may ask the body what message it has for you. (Let the body answer—don't allow your mind to jump in with an answer.) Sometimes just being aware of the particular energy from that level can help you see into that level with greater understanding and clarity.

Function – When you have developed the expansion, which is an opening up, and the awareness of the particular body, then you should learn to consciously function more from that level. Watch for pictures or feelings which may appear when you are working with a particular level. If you do not understand the pictures, become them, feel them. For instance, if you see a mountain, be the mountain, or if you see a bird, be the bird. You might also want to imitate any action the bird was performing. This helps you to interpret and understand it. As you develop these bodies more you will learn to see psychically and pick up messages from these levels. There is much information to be gained from each level as the development increases.

Different stones have different properties and can be healing, strengthening, or lift the consciousness in our bodies.*

NATURE

Nature has long been a special place for meditators. For some, woods or natural places suffice. For others, meditative gardens are designed and built to enhance the expanded state of consciousness.

Even a place with a few plants can help bring the energies of nature into the meditator's consciousness.

Meditation can be practiced just by being in nature or in relating to aspects of nature. Following are meditations which can help us relate to this very important part of our planet.

Meditation 1

Choose a tree. Really look at it, be aware of it, and then feel your consciousness go into the tree. Be aware of the tree's consciousness, be one with the tree. Focus your full attention until you experience a

---

* Note: Rock sets are available from Orange Eye Company, Box 456, Melbourne, AR 72556, or you may purchase them separately at a rock shop.

merging of yourself with the tree. What do you experience? Then let yourself feel that you are friends and co-inhabitors of this planet.

You may wish to do the same with a bird, animal, insect, or plant.

Meditation 2 — Meditations Upon the Seasons
by Helen McMahan

We humans seem to have an annual cycle which mimics the cycle of our planet. We go through a dormant winter, dreaming to choose the seeds to plant in our lives' gardens. We plant those seeds, and as they germinate they bring an experience of emotional uncertainty as we wonder which will sprout within our lives. Then comes the Sun of springtime to warm them, and the seeds of our dreams start to sprout into realities. Just as in our physical gardens, we must learn to prune and weed, making difficult decisions about what we should grow and where we will choose to direct our energies. Summertime arrives with a riotous growth. All of our dreaming seeds come into being. All our creativity is manifested within our relationships, careers, hobbies, arts, and personal development. Then comes the fall when we gather in our harvest, evaluating what our dreams have created, where to fit the fruits of our growth into our value structure, and share what we have learned about living with others.

This annual cycle of growth follows a cycle of dares which Genevieve Lewis Paulson suggested to me many years ago. Very simply and yet quite profoundly, she said that human life was based upon three dares. We must *dare* to dream, *dare* to take risks, and *dare* to do whatever is necessary to make

---

* Printed with permission, Helen McMahan, Orbis Farm, Louisville, KY and Mauckport, IN.

our dreams come true. The winter time of Earth's annual cycle is definitely a time to dare to dream. During spring, we must dare to take risks in choosing which of our dreams to follow. In summer, we dare to do whatever it takes to cultivate those dreams, manifesting them into reality within our lives. Finally, in the fall, we integrate our year and fit our dreams, our risk-taking, and all of our work into the ever-expanding being which we are.

Winter: A Time to Dream

Stretch out luxuriously into a state of relaxation, opening your physical body to free-flowing energy, will, and power. Toes stretch out and go limp with relaxation; fingers uncurl and release your force into the environment surrounding you. Your inner observer awakes and begins to notice your body breathing. The nostrils flare as they draw in the life-producing air, with the oxygen feeding each cell within your body. The exhalation releases toxins and disease from each one of those cells. And the being who is the "I" within you watches this interchange between your body and the environment. Peace, calm, and acceptance seep into your relaxed, open, flowing body.

Who are you? What do you want? What do you want to do? Who do you want to be? Let your awareness sink deeper and deeper into yourself. This is a new year, a new beginning, a time of great promise and excitement, the seeding time of the year when dreams are spun. How do you want this year to unfold for you in your personal spiritual journey? Relax your mind; do not forceably look for answers. Listen to yourself. Wait, watch, attune yourself to what is yearning to manifest in your life.

Resting against the Earth, feel yourself floating into a brand new space, entirely open to new dreams and new plans. As you take in another breath, follow it with your awareness as it draws you deeper and deeper inside yourself. Let yourself travel with your imagination deeply into your mind. Let that imagination loose to dream. Release any of your ordinary mind "sets." Set aside all of those restrictions you habitually have placed upon yourself, all of the things you usually say and think that limit who you are, what you can do, who you can become. Expand out of your past patterns, letting loose all of the old, safe, familiar attitudes. As you float deeper and deeper into your mind, feel yourself expanding. Experience with your imagination a stretching, daring, soaring feeling exploding within you. Stretch into a brand-new concept of yourself.

Let yourself dream! What far-out things can you imagine yourself doing this year? What adventures can your imagination create? What marvels can your mind, creativity, and will *intend* to manifest?

Spring: Time to Dare

Close your eyes and sit very straight and still, relaxing upon the foundations of your physical body. Begin to closely focus your attention upon the very familiar act of breathing. Observe the way your body works to breathe. First your lungs empty and you pause for a moment to feel that emptiness. Then you open yourself consciously, really allowing "opening" to occur. Joyously your nostrils dilate to drink in that next breath. Be aware that it is not only oxygen, nitrogen, and a few other trace elements which you are gratefully inviting into your being, but also a magical, humming energy substance that constitutes life, a substance the Hindus name "prana." Watch the breath fill your nose and sinus cavities. Sniff to sense the coolness and scent of the breath. Direct part of that breath up through your forehead into your brain, part of it into the back of your throat and head and then consciously follow the remainder of that breath directly down into your chest and lungs. Observe your lungs expand, inflating your chest, stretching your ribs, expanding your belly. Hold the breath within you. With that in-held breath, feel full and imagine the millions of sparkling droplets of life, of prana, moving into every crevice of your being. Begin to exhale as slowly and deliberately as is possible. Let yourself consciously release toxins which are the beginnings of disease. Tell your body that it is really all right to let go. As you hold the breath outside of your body for a few seconds, directly experience what it means to feel empty, hollow, yet expectant.

Continue to breathe rhythmically while you bear in mind that by consciously focusing upon the rhythm of your breathing, you actually increase the amount of life energy you possess. Inhale as you count to four, hold your breath inside while you count to four, exhale slowly and deliberately as you count to four, retain that hollow emptiness, holding your breath outside of your body, and count to four. Create a square with your breathing cycle. Observe your body repeating this cycle over and over again. Consciousness continues to focus upon the fact that you are building the vitality of your life by welcoming in the sparkling droplets of vitality contained within the breath.

The cycle of breath triggers our awareness of many other cycles in which we exist: the cycle of happiness and sadness, of sickness and health, of life and death, and the cycle of the annual trip Earth takes around the sun, the cycle of our seasons.

Just sitting, breathing, being intently aware of that breath, allow everything else to become still. Watch your nostrils dilate and feel the spring winds enter, while you remain totally relaxed. There is nothing to do, nothing to look for. Just breathe and relax, holding onto that breath as if it were the thread of Ariadne guiding you through the maze of your consciousness. Keep the awareness focused, breathing in and breathing out. Stillness settles within the mind as you watch the stream of sensations and thoughts pass through you. Do not follow, do not become caught up. Just breathe, holding onto the sensation of breathing there at your nostrils. Witness life itself flow through you. There is nothing to ask, nothing to remember. Just breathe in the springtime of your life.

Summer: A Time to Do
"Creativity"

Close your eyes and let yourself sink down deeply inside of your richness, your fullness, your vastness. Become aware of this physical body as a hollow tube open to the complete and unimpeded flow of energy from your earthly mother to your divinity and from your Heavenly Father down deep into your humanity. Watch this flow begin at the soles of your feet and move without interruption or impediment all the way through you to fountain out of the crown of your head; all of your earthiness, with its know-how, its ability to make and to manifest erupting through your spiritual center like tangible bands of energy. Allow that material earthiness to mix and dance with the divine energy, that grace of God which forever surrounds us.

Open up your spiritual center at the crown to allow divinity to flow, again without block or diversion, down through the hollow tube which is your body, to blend with the humanity which you represent. Watch this energy twirling through you, let it flow, accept and understand, for this moment in time, your incredible destiny. Recognize within the blending of earthly and heavenly energies that we humans alone, of all manifestation, are capable of such a mixture.

Experience the vastness of the universe which you are, and begin to sense how this vastness mirrors the colossal expanse of the entire created universe. Let your heart tremble with love and gratitude at this pouring, flowing, mixing, and blending of energies. You are unique. There is no other soul within the universe exactly like yours. Allow a sense of your eternal soul to stir within you with desires and images of your deepest longings, your most powerful yearnings. What would your soul love to create with this lifetime? These soul desires and images begin to shape and focus all of this rushing flow of divinity and humanity mingling within you.

Allow your conscious mind to begin to accept these images, these yearnings and longings, and start to shape them into thoughts, plans of creativity. In this magical season of summer, let your mind begin to formulate a plan. What are some of the images you would like to manifest in the days to come? Open your mind to listen to your soul. Focus upon the next month, the next year, the next ten years. Dreams for the next decade must be crafted now. Let creation emanate from you.

Fall: A Time to Integrate

Stretch yourself out and close your eyes. Let yourself go! Soften up the neck and feel your breath whoosh through that area. Open your chest to a nice stretch expansion, settling your awareness within your heart. Be very soft, open, and vulnerable in this upper chest. Feel how warm and understanding this softness allows you to be. Breathe very softly, very gently, but very deeply. Experience how good it feels to expand those chest muscles and actually make room inside for your heart and all that it symbolizes. Compassion flowing, taking your time, being tactful, being understanding, feeling empathy, experiencing bonds of love and pity, fun and irritation, with all those other human beings out there just like you. What has happened to your soft, loving heart lately? What changes have come about within it? What new insights, deeper wisdoms, gentle knowings have crept into your awareness this year? Relax the chest to let your heart whisper to you of all the compassionate newness which has penetrated your life.

Release and relax more heavily into the floor beneath you. Allow your awareness to sink into the incredible strength and solidity of your spinal cord. Feel that base, the flexibility of it, the vulnerability of it. Experience a sense of stiffening, of bracing yourself to withstand the winds of life. Feel yourself steel yourself to handle life, to meet the blows, to follow through, to continue putting one foot in front of the other and make your imprint, knowing that it was meant to be and hence it is vital and very important. Feel your will singing through your nerves, strengthening your resolutions, backing you up, firming your motivation. What newness has occurred to you lately within your will, your stick-to-itism, your determination and belief in yourself, and trust in the universe? What has happened to your guts, your heart, your backbone? How have you changed and grown in the handling of this year of manifesting the seeds of your dreams?

Relax and just breathe. Let go of the steel of your backbone and find your breath expanding your body at the sides of your ribs, the shoulder joints in front of your body, at the hip joints in the front of your body. Melting and breathing, expand and soften yourself. Be aware of the curve at the side of your neck and open up to the high self within you, the eternal within, the never-ending stream of consciousness which is the very soul of your being. What sorts of newness have come into your life from this soul? What new spiritual insights have you become aware of during this year? How has your perception of your personality expanded with a spiritual, soul-level element? How have some of your life's goals come under question? Gather this information together now and acknowledge to yourself the growth of your spirit.

Lift your breath now, spreading your awareness to your heart and the top of your head. Feel your connections with an incredible light of love which is other-worldly, which can only be designated as divine. What else is out there? What newness is coming into your being about your deepest beliefs? Those beliefs in something higher than you, greater, more powerful, much more knowing, gently and incredibly wise, and very loving? Filled with a loving compassion that is bigger than even your facile brain can conceive, what new beliefs have come into your being? What new glimmers of faith, what new tinges of unconditional love have begun to distill into your everyday consciousness and are now asking you to incorporate into every fiber of the fabric of your life?

FOCUS ON THE HEAVENS

Planets

You don't have to understand astrology in order to tune into the energy of the Sun, Moon, and planets. Each one has a main vibration which, far away as they may be, will still affect us.

Meditation

As you meditate on each heavenly body, let your body be filled with the Sun, Moon, or planet's energy. Be in an open meditation for a few minutes. What information comes to you? Since each of the planets, the Sun, and the Moon have energies which can feel negative to you, it is important to ask any negativity to turn to positive for you. It is helpful to learn to turn all energy to a positive force for you, whether it comes from the heavens or someplace else.

Write down what information you receive so that you can work with it more some other time. (Note: You may only want to do three or four of the planets at a time, as the energy can be quite strong.)

- Sun: rapturous, life giving, expansive, hopeful.

- Moon: goes into inner self, broody, new ideas.

- Venus: feminine, soft, artistic, love.

- Mercury: quickness, mental, not always stable, connective.

- Earth: evolution, development, balance of earth and heavens, balance of nature and God, stability (slower moving than Mercury), practicality.

- Mars: hard, mental, forceful, can be warlike.

- Jupiter: expansive (similar to Sun), uplifting, pushes higher, dreams.

- Saturn: pushes downward to ground, focuses, basic, practicality.

- Uranus: explosive, impulsive, opens to higher energies, opens doors, affects Kundalini.

- Neptune: no boundaries, opens to other possibilities, problem solving, illusive, very spiritual, or very dark.

- Pluto: inner worlds, transformation, can be dark if not able to handle and transform, uncovers hidden possibilities

You will note that some planets seem to have opposite purposes. Below are some examples:

The Sun deals primarily with expansion and the outer world while the Moon turns the energy inward to the inner self and the inner world.

Other opposites are:

- Venus and Mars
- Jupiter and Saturn
- Mercury and Earth
- Pluto (inward) and Uranus (outward)

Meditation on Planet Energies

The following meditation may help you balance these energies. A few minutes on each is sufficient in the beginning.

1. Ask to feel the energies of the Sun and Moon in your body at one time. Expand inward and outward, otherwise it may be uncomfortable and compressing.

2. Ask to feel the energies of Venus and Mars in your body. You may wish to be aware of the heart and waist for Venus, shoulders and brains for Mars. This can help you feel very balanced, polarity-wise, and give a strong sense of peaceful power.

3. Ask to feel the energies of Mercury and Earth in your body. You may wish to be aware of the head for Mercury and the feet and tailbone for Earth. This can give more substance to your communications and practicality to your thoughts.

4. Ask to feel Jupiter and Saturn in your body. You need to expand outward and inward (as you did for the Sun and Moon) to get the most benefit. Strong leadership, determination, and direction can come from this combination.

5. Ask to feel Uranus and Pluto in your body. This is another inner and outer combination. Treat them the same as you did the Sun and Moon, and Jupiter and Saturn. Feel the chest and head for Uranus, and the belly area for Pluto. If you don't feel too stable this might not help, as it is a rather volatile combination.

Breathe gently into the energies and watch them. Let loose of your solar plexus so you don't become nauseous. This exercise helps you feel the power of change energy in your body. How would you like to direct it?

STARS AND GALAXIES

Some persons like to meditate on the energy of stars and/or galaxies. They, too, have great energy which does reach the Earth. You may pick a certain galaxy or star and ask to be filled with its vibrations. Then be in an open meditation and allow insights to come to you.

Following are some stars, constellations, and galaxies you may wish to meditate upon. It does not matter if you do not have information on them. The vibration will still be there. You might want to get an astronomy book and study these power centers further.

Stars

Some stars you might want to meditate on include: Sirius, Procyon, Alpha Centauri, Ceti, Altair, Vega, Betelguese, Regulus, Arcturus, and our Sun.

Constellations

Some constellations you may wish to meditate upon are Aries, Taurus, Gemini, Cancer, Leo, Virgo, Libra, Scorpio, Sagittarius, Capricorn, Aquarius, Pisces, Cassiopeia, Pegasus, Ursa Minor, and Ursa Major.

Galaxies

Galaxies to meditate on include Sombrero (NGC 4594); NGC 3031; The great Andromeda Galaxy (M31=NGC 222); Milky Way (ours); NGC 3115; The Large Magellenic Cloud; NGC 2525; and NGC 2523.

The Moon

The Moon has a particularly strong influence on us and its effect changes with its cycles. As you learn to work with the Moon's energies you will speed your efforts.

Full Moon

Full Moon energies help us to cleanse our three lower bodies, physical, emotional, and mental. Persons can become quite emotional during this period. They can also become quite irrational which is a mental body dysfunction. The physical body can be "out of sorts" or heavy. If much of the cleansing is already done for these bodies, or if you give special time to use these energies to do what needs to be done, then the energy will become "pure." It can then be used quite productively in various ways—it is free for your use.

Full Moon Meditation

Be in a comfortable position. Open your mind to Full Moon energies—let them be balanced in your brain area. Bless any problems which come to mind.

Release them for the moment and let your brain be peaceful for awhile.

Alternately tighten and relax the belly area a few times. Then with a relaxed belly (emotional) area, feel the Moon's energies strengthening it. Release any problems for the moment and let the belly area be peaceful.

Stretch your body well, relax it, and then stretch again. Release tensions and allow the energy to come in as strength. Meditate on projects you would like to tackle.

New Moon

New Moon energies are strongest about five days before and after the New Moon, when there is almost no Sun reflection from the Moon on us. This allows the energies from the galaxy to reach us more powerfully, as they are not diffused by the sun. These are called galactic energies, and do not affect as heavily persons who are not using their higher bodies in a concentrated manner. These energies can bring in great strength. Meditations on higher planes will be greatly enhanced during this period. Insights from higher levels or planes are quite likely to come during this period. Over-meditating during this time can bring in too much galactic energy, which can leave you feeling like your mind is blown.

New Moon Meditation

Be in a comfortable position. Relax the physical body. Let yourself feel open and balanced, inside and out. Be aware. Does some new healing or strength want to come in?

Relax the belly (emotional) area. Feel your emotions being lifted up and becoming expansive. What higher emotions want to express themselves?

Shake your head gently a few times. Be aware of energy inside and outside of your head; especially open up the area above your head. Ask for new information. Be receptive and give the energy time to form into words, concepts, or pictures.

Have the feeling of floating, being in touch with higher dimensions. Ask for new information to come in. (You may ask for it in a specific area, if you wish.)

7

FOCUS ON ENERGIES

We are filled and surrounded with many energies all of the time. Learning to separate these and use them for centering, lifting one's consciousness, and becoming aware of messages can be very helpful. Colors and numbers are manifestations of particular vibrations and have their own purposes. The rainbow colors, especially, relate to the main frequencies of energy which are important in our daily lives and our growth. The use of them in meditation can help center and direct a person.

COLORS AND WHITE LIGHT

White Light as a Shield

Many individuals dedicated to spiritual growth employ the technique of surrounding themselves with white light as a means of protection from negative influences and as a way of enhancing a state of spiritual awareness. To this end the white light works extremely well. It's very spiritual and very protective. Unfortunately, it may work too well! As a means of protection, the white light may shield you from negative energies or feedback from others, which can help you in understanding yourself as well as others. This is especially true when the energies you are receiving have a lower vibratory level (such as negativity) than your own white light. This means negative energies sent by others would be blocked from your awareness. At this point you might say, "Fine, that's exactly the type of protection I want!" However, it is here that the white light becomes a two-edged sword, cutting positively on one side and negatively on the other. As a result, the white light may actually slow down and inhibit your spiritual growth and personal development. (See figure 2.)

Negative feedback helps us to modify our behavior as we learn to relate to others. This is an essential aspect of establishing and developing personal relationships with those around us. If this is blocked, we will not be aware of our own inappropriate behavior. Thus, the surrounding of the white light may inhibit the understanding of ourselves which is one of the very foundations of spiritual growth.

Filling Self in White Light

The better approach is to fill yourself with a white light. This helps to strengthen you so that you can understand and handle energies better. It does not create blocks. Instead you will be filled with, and radiating, light (see figure 3). Use the white light gradually so you build up your ability to use it.

Problems of Insufficient Development

Many people are not sufficiently developed in spiritual awareness to use white light correctly. White light, when diffused through a prism, manifests distinct shades of red, orange, yellow, green, blue, purple, and red-violet. Each of these colors represents a particular frequency of energy which we use in our daily lives. If we have not developed the ability to use each color properly, then we are likewise unable to use the white light properly. In this sense, the laws of spirit are similar to the laws of mathematics and physics, i.e., the whole is equal to the sum of the parts. If the parts (individual colors) are imperfect, then it must follow that the whole

Figure 2

Excessive white light around a person becomes a barrier to interaction with others.

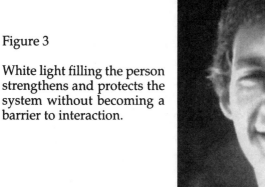

Figure 3

White light filling the person strengthens and protects the system without becoming a barrier to interaction.

(Photo by Pete Beevers)

(white light) will also be imperfect. The degree of imperfection in the separate colors limits the power, strength, and usefulness of the white light.

When an individual who has not mastered the separate colors attempts to use the white light for protection and healing it is similar to 220-volt energy running through a 110-volt body. Circuits break, fuses blow, and the white light may turn into darkened negativity. White light in its negative form can manifest as spiritual pride, closed mindedness, and rigidity in attitudes, with the overall result being a lower level of spiritual development.

When the individual is truly developed and has mastered the component colors, he or she is able to assimilate and use pure white light in its fullest form. Protection, healing, and spiritual growth will follow.

COLORS: POSITIVE AND NEGATIVE EFFECTS

The colors representing the major frequencies of energy and their positive and negative effects are listed in the chart that follows.

Chart 2 POSITIVE AND NEGATIVE EFFECTS OF COLOR	
Color	**Positive Effects**
Red	Pure energy for action, ability to flow with task, ability to accomplish, joy of life.
Orange	Excitement, intensity, active mentality, more directed than red for getting things done.
Yellow	Sunny feelings, high mentality, abundance of ideas, open-minded, expansive.
Green	Healing, peaceful, warmth, enjoyment of nature, desire to get into the "swing" of life and be where the action is, desire to live life fully.

(Chart 2, cont'd)	
Blue	Selfless devotion, faith, feeling of spirit, calm, peaceful, understanding, compassionate, intuitive, appreciative.
Purple	Expansion, secure, passion for life and being.
Red-violet	Reaching out, aspiring (can be spiritual or other aspirations), understanding of things to be attained, yearning, ability to change from status quo.
White	All-ness, one-ness, secure with the growth process.
Color	**Negative Effects**
Red	Anger, frustration, a heaviness, dullness (because energy does not move), evil, stuckness, desire to lash out or to hurt others.
Orange	Sickly, inability to cope, pomposity, self-importance, worry, poor digestion.
Yellow	Prejudice, rigid thinking patterns, confusion, sad , despair, fear, perplexity, paranoia, inability to think clearly.
Green	Anger, jealousy, desire to push people away, tendency to worry, illness, despair, mistrust, reclusive, immobilized, tendency to turn nose up at things, inability to relate.
Blue	Pushy, overbearing, fanatical or dogmatic ideologies, great rigidity in devotion, self-righteous.
Purple	Bigoted, bold, heavy, solemn, structured, overly inclined to ceremony and ritual, passion for self.
Red violet	Cruelty, desire to control others, loss of self-control, vengeful, arrogance in judgment, inability to perceive clearly, horror.
White	Gray, feel small, inability to handle positive energies, defenseless, powerless, desire to turn to dark forces, feeling of being pressured and put upon.

Meditation Exercises for Development

By meditating with these rainbow colors you can discover which ones have not been mastered. A feeling of discomfort or an inability to concentrate on a particular color indicates you need additional work with that specific energy. The following is a basic rainbow meditation.

First step—be in a comfortable position, preferably with the back straight. Relax and loosen your body. Fill yourself with each color in turn and hold each one for approximately one minute. As you work to bring the colors into your system, begin with the lighter shades of the colors, as this will allow you to experience their positive side initially. Do not use the colors in their dark or muddy hues until you feel comfortable with their lighter shades, because much negativity can be released from darker shades.

If you cannot see or feel the color, then imagine it. Energy follows imagination. When you have finished with each of the colors—red, orange, yellow, green, blue, purple, and red-violet—then fill yourself with the white radiance. Hold the radiance for about a minute, then stop and stretch.

As you develop, you may wish to increase your meditation time in each color. Be careful, your increased time should be gradual and comfortable. As you feel competent with the energy, you may wish to hold each color for two minutes, then three, etc. As you meditate, always keep an open mind to allow messages and understanding to come through.

Your meditation may be enhanced by placing a crystal or prism in a position where sunlight will diffuse through it. This will help you see and experience the richness and brightness of each color.

This basic rainbow meditation can help in centering and grounding, and can also leave you feeling more in touch with your destiny energies.

By working consistently with the rainbow meditation you should find the following:

- As you develop, the white light will glow within. The white light will then be a protective, healing force, without being a block or shield from others.

- Your overall growth and development will be much faster and easier.

- The rainbow exercise is an excellent means of cleansing, centering, and toning up for further meditations.

- You can use this particular meditation for higher development by seeing the colors as fire. Keep in mind, however, that seeing the colors as fire brings in much higher energy patterns. Thus, the fire colors should only be used after you have developed to where you can handle the higher frequencies of energy.

As we move further and further into the Aquarian Age, the energies will become stronger and more difficult to deal with. Because of this, it is imperative that we learn to work with and use the energies properly. As you meditate with the various colors, you will discover other ways for working with the energies, which will increase your personal and spiritual growth. As you do this you will move toward that time when you will discover that mystical spiritual secret—we are not just physical humans, we are prisms of the universe reflecting the energies of God!

NUMEROLOGY

Numerology has long been recognized as having great influence over us and for us. The vibration of each number affects certain areas of our personalities and our lives. It is not necessary to have training in this for the numbers to become effective tools for growth. The numbers do mean specific things to individuals, as well as having general meanings for all. As you do the meditations, the information that is most relevant to you will appear.

Meditation 1

Fill yourself with each number in turn. For instance, imagine the form of a giant "1" in your body, then a giant "2" and so on. Allow yourself to tune into the vibrations of each number. As you do this, let your mind ramble; many times messages or new awareness will come through (this is openness, receptivity). To begin, use the numbers 1 through 9, 0, 11, 22 and 33. What do the energies of these numbers mean to you?

Meditation 2

If you would like to work more with the numbers, you may wish to purchase a good book on numerology. Using the book on numerology, find out the numerological vibrations for your name.

1. What does this tell you about yourself? Be open to new information.

2. Feel your name in your body without the number. Does it correspond to the numerology feeling? Be open to new information.

3. Fill yourself with the total number for your name and the feeling of your name. Be open to new information.

THE ALPHABET

Use the same procedure as you did for numbers, only use the letters in the alphabet.

HUMOR AND WISDOM

Meditators sooner or later have humorous symbols or puns appear. It seems the higher a person develops, the more humor occurs.

Since humor on the higher levels usually involves interaction with different concepts, it can also contain a core of wisdom. Following is a meditation which uses humor as a vehicle for greater understanding.

*Twentieth Century Wisdom**
by David Bahn

Stretch out or sit comfortably . . .

Take deep peaceful breaths . . .

This is a meditation about wisdom . . .

The ancients had ways of recording wisdom . . . The Ten Commandments were on stone tablets, the Torah was on scrolls, and even paintings on cave walls recorded the wisdom of the time.

The twentieth century has its own way of recording wisdom . . . the T-Shirt and the bumper sticker . . .

"We can do Magic"

"Beam me up, Scotty"

"Gee, Toto I don't think we're in Kansas anymore"

Or the one that states well the relation of man to man . . .

"Be careful, I drive the way you do."

---

* Used with permission, David Bahn, Willowend, Jacksonville, FL.

Imagine you are walking down a narrow street lined with small shops . . . a book shop, and over there a rock and crystal dealer. You stop in front of "Evolutionary T-Shirts." The windows are filled with samples . . . in many colors and multi-colors.

Walk in and look over the racks of T-shirts. Some of the ones already printed that stand out are . . .

"The age of Eggquarius" (picture of surprised chicken and an egg).

"Be kind to me, I'm a Pisces."

"Fly Astral, the airline of the Stars."

"Arms are for hugging, not war."

Not all T-shirts are printed. Some are in colors . . . bright or plain. They come in all sizes, or one size fits all. A clerk with an airbrush is ready to print whatever message you choose . . .

You work your way through the racks and find your T-shirt. What color is it? What size do you choose . . . Big and floppy or tight-hugging? Does it have a message? Boldly printed or quietly discreet?

At the register you see a rack of bumper stickers. Which one do you pick out? Will it go on your car or in your desk drawer?

You pay for your purchases and walk out, making a note to come back on a different day . . . in a different mood perhaps . . .

Laughter weakens form and structure within each of us. A good laugh stops all work. When the laughing is completed, a person can sense less tension, less structure in the body. It opens the system to more expansive, relaxed ways of being. Laughter could be considered as an active form of meditation because it will do a number of the same things for a person that meditation will. It is helpful to have a good laugh several times a day to reduce stress.

NON-FOCUSED MEDITATIONS

In a non-focused meditation it is easy in the beginning for thoughts to wander, to remember things you haven't done, or to plan to do tomorrow. I find it very helpful at the beginning of a non-focused meditation to let all thoughts come wandering through. I write down those I wish to deal with at a later time. Some of these thoughts have been waiting a long time to get into consciousness and they need to be heard. After about ten minutes I am usually cleared out and ready to just "be."

Sometimes in the stillness of non-focused meditation, spiritual experiences occur or there may be an enlightenment on some subject. Appreciate the experience, make your notes (it is so easy to forget these things), and continue.

Non-focusing is sometimes difficult for the beginners. It is also very easy to open to lower astral influences if you are not in a clear state. If you wish to try this form, there are several ways that I can suggest which will help you get to higher levels and thus be protected. Below are some variations of the non-focused meditation that may be helpful.

Prayer Meditation

Be in a prayer state, feel yourself lifted up, and then just be in the prayer energy. Prayers may arise spontaneously from you, insights may come in, energies may move significantly in your body, or nothing may happen. If you continue this particular exercise over a period of time, you will find you are more centered, intuitive, and more aware.

Peace Meditation

Open yourself up, relax, let peace and calm penetrate your system. Then become aware of your body, your feelings, your thoughts, and your spirit. Tune into the energies in you. Be one with them and let them speak to you. Let whatever wants to come to your attention do so.

Observing Thoughts and Feelings Meditation

Either sit or lie down in a comfortable position. Let your thoughts or feelings appear, don't stop them or push them away, just let them float on by. Let your shoulders relax; this will help you be unattached to the process.

You may wish to make notes of things you wish to remember or explore further some other time.

Blanking the Mind Meditation

This is a state of utter stillness. No thoughts intruding. There are several ways to help achieve this:

1. Focus on the pineal gland (center of the head—see figure 10). Don't do this for over three to four minutes in the beginning, as it may release too much spiritual energy for the body to handle well. (Sometimes information from higher levels comes to consciousness.)

2. Focus on the center of each eyebrow. This slows or stops thinking. Do this for one to two minutes so your brain can calm down.

CLOSING

There are many different books and tapes available with meditations for those who wish to further expand their understanding of this energy. It also could be very helpful for you if you would design some of your own meditations. Be creative with this energy, experiment, work with it. You will find types of meditations which best suit you to use for your basic meditative practice. Then periodically use different forms so that you do not become stuck in your practice. Meditation can open new dimensions, new worlds, new ways of being.

8

EXTRASENSORY PERCEPTIONS—THE THREE C'S

E xtrasensory perception is the term given to the awareness of things beyond what our so-called normal senses can perceive. The New Testament, several times, quotes Jesus as saying, "If you have eyes to see, then see. If you have ears to hear, then hear." I believe this to be referring to these extra awarenesses, these extra perceptions that we are called to develop. Some terms used for these perceptions are energy, premonition, universal consciousness, intuitions, hunches, psychosomatic influences, higher self, unconscious, soul level, creative flow, sensing, still small voice within, guides, angels, and God. These terms relate to different levels of perception and different sources.

THE THREE C'S

Clairvoyance, clairaudience, and clairsentience are three of the main psychic or paranormal abilities which persons have. They may develop seemingly in a spontaneous way as the person's energy patterns change, or as they experience growth. Through certain exercises the development of these abilities may be increased in clarity, and understanding of their use may be enhanced. As we get farther and farther into the New Age, there are increases in energies which will cause us to have these experiences more frequently.

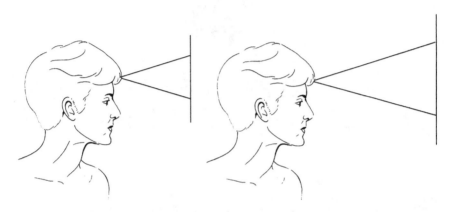

Figure 4	Figure 5
The developed clairvoyant can project images from the psychic eyes onto an energy screen.	Very highly developed clairvoyants may focus images further out to enhance detail.

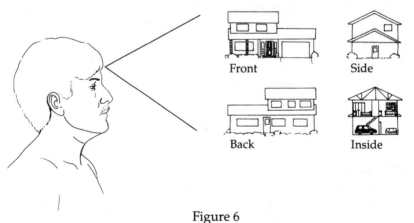

Figure 6
Using mind power, objects may be turned or entered into for a more complete viewing.

CLAIRVOYANCE

Clairvoyance (clear seeing) is the name given to psychic sight. In the beginning a person may see clouds of color, vague scenes, or half-formed symbols. Further development brings vivid color, detailed symbols, pictures, scenes, or geometric shapes. Things which are seen from very high spiritual levels will appear as though there is great light on them and in them.

Some people "see" through feeling or sensing. This is valid as well.

There are three forms of seeing—symbolic, literal, or a combination of symbolic and literal. When seeing literally, a person may view the events correctly, but sometimes have difficulty understanding where they fit in or what is actually happening. When seeing symbolically, and if able to interpret the symbols, one has a tendency to get the meaning more easily, but not necessarily the details of how it will happen. To see both literally and symbolically can be very confusing, unless you have developed understanding of paranormal sight and then the result is much clearer than either totally symbolic or totally literal. If you see symbolically, know that everything you see is correct. However, the interpretation you give may be totally incorrect! It takes practice and understanding to develop good interpretation skills.

A person may see something which has happened that was unknown to him or her (postcognition), or they may see something that is happening someplace else (remote viewing), or may happen in the future (precognition). Since the visions or pictures come from many areas, it can be confusing. For instance, if you see something symbolically, there may be trouble in understanding the symbolism. Since symbols come from the feeling level, you need to put the symbol into the feeling level in order to understand it.

Also, you may see something out of context. Most visions are out of context and you do not understand what it means for you or why it is happening. Most persons truly do not understand until the event occurs, then they remember the vision and it gives support, direction, and clarification while the event is happening.

It is possible to see things that are happening someplace else and feel that it is symbolic.

Eventually, as a person develops, it is possible to feel the different energy of the literal or symbolic picture. Sometimes visions or pictures come from our fantasy world, and, if you recognize them as coming from the fantasy world, it can help you understand either your hidden desires or potentials which are trying to come through.

In clairvoyance, a person may see geometric shapes, colors or light. This is a way of seeing from the high mental plane. Again, becoming these geometric shapes, colors, or light will help in understanding their meanings.

Some pictures may appear very vividly in technicolor, or it may be that it appears as if a brilliant light was shining upon the scene. It may also be very dim and barely seen. Some persons do not actually see, but they sense that they see something. There is a sense that there is a symbol, and that counts as well. Each persons "sees" in different ways.

Whatever picture you see is the most probable of the future events, and if you do not like what you see, you can ask if there are alternatives or ask to see alternatives. You may even ask what would strengthen a possible future or what would weaken it.

As development increases, a person may begin to see the following things:

- Auras, which are color manifestations of energy around persons, plants, and animals; in fact, all living things.

- Astral forms, such as ghosts.

- More complex or intricate pictures, more highly developed and intricate geometric forms, thought forms, the Akashic Records (records of past and future lives).

Highly Developed Clairvoyance

In highly developed clairvoyance the following things are possible:

- X-ray vision (actually seeing into persons or objects).

- Greater depth of sight and control of Akashic Record viewing.

- Seeing of spiritual beings and symbols.

- Seeing energy in its pure form (some will look like rain and others have varying shapes). The seeing of germs or minute objects.

- Being able to see into the manifestation process; to see how things happened in the past and present, and are forming the future. It is possible to see energy patterns between persons, such as karmic forces or present connections.

- As some persons develop, they may find that they begin to see pictures with their eyes open. These pictures will appear approximately three feet in front of them (see figure 4). It is similar to an energy screen which allows you to project what you are seeing from your psychic eyes onto its surface. The picture becomes larger and more detailed.

Greater development allows a person to project the picture further, thus enhancing the detail (see figure 5). If persons around you were evolved and trained enough, it would be possible for them to also see the images on the wall from your projections.

With the power of your mind, it is possible to turn the visualization sideways or around so it can be viewed from all sides. You can also open it up and see inside (see figure 6).

The manifestation process is happening in us all of the time. As all of our probable futures come together—energies from our astrological influences, the energies from our past lives, our hopes, dreams, our spiritual development, the energies of the places in which we live, and energies from friends, their hopes and dreams for us—all of these things work together and create our probable futures. It can help us to make better choices, it can help us to understand what is happening to us, and it can help us to transmute energy that is emerging in a negative form into something that's more positive.

How to Develop Clairvoyance

One way of developing this ability is to close your physical eyes and ask to see pictures of things. You should start with things that don't really matter, such as asking what you might want to wear the next day, or asking about some foods your body would like to have. It is best to start this way because, if you get into a question that could be too emotional, such as seeing a picture of your destiny or how a relationship will work out, you could get overly involved in it. Then your desires and emotions would color what you would see and, although your picture would be correct, you would not realize that you were interpreting or seeing your desires and emotions rather than seeing actuality. Be careful not to jump to conclusions regarding the meanings. Try to keep your emotions and thoughts out of it.

As you see the pictures, whether literal, symbolic, or a combination of literal and symbolic, become them. Become the symbols. Give yourself plenty of time to adjust to the energy of the symbol and let it speak to you. Let yourself be in a nonattached attitude. It will allow you to receive information in a clearer form. It is like pretending you don't really care. This frees the energy from your desires and fears. Peaceful, deep breathing should aid in this release. Sometimes a person gets so excited over seeing something, he or she forgets to take in sufficient air, and this can cause a block in further receiving and interpreting. In some cases a person will get other symbols as an answer, and this can be very frustrating. In this case, the person was probably too attached to the answer to get the information straight, and it thus forms symbolically. You also may like to try asking the symbol what it means, because sometimes answers will come in words.

As mentioned above, sometimes visions may be so out of context that it is difficult to get understanding. You cannot see where it would fit in or the meaning it has. The main purpose for this type of vision is to help prepare your system for the coming change. Even if you don't comprehend it consciously, it is fully understood on other levels. Be aware that you may see something which will not happen for another four or five years. It doesn't usually come labeled, "for four or five years in the future." It doesn't generally tell the circumstances surrounding the particular event. What may seem scary, or fearful, or overwhelming at the time you see it, may feel perfectly normal and appropriate when it happens.

Because of the confusion that surrounds these gifts, many times persons shut them off rather than learn to work with them. Patience is helpful with this. If the meaning does not come to your full consciousness until the event has happened, it can still give you great courage. You saw this, therefore there is something special about it. It has a very confirming aspect.

You may see pictures in your head, or you may be one of those persons who project the pictures out several inches or many feet in front of the forehead. Either way is valid. Some persons see only in the psychic eye areas. Some have panoramic vision, incorporating the entire forehead. Some may have a sense of seeing with the entire body. It varies with development and with which chakras are open most. Some persons will see radiant white light. This is associated with spiritual levels. Quite often with this it is difficult to discern a message, although the more developed you are, the more you will receive information from the spiritual or radiant white light as well. A flat, white light is a lower level of spiritual energy.

When these exercises are first done, a sense of openness and relaxation may be felt in the forehead or in the entire head. If they are overdone it may result in headaches or nervousness. There may also be a release of emotional and mental blocks at a rate faster than a person cares to deal with. In such cases, it is best to stop the practice and do something entirely different for awhile. Also, be aware that sometimes when you are seeing things very vividly, there may be later times when your visions may be dim. Do not worry about this. Different events have more power, different thoughts or feelings have more power. Intensity varies in what appears to you.

When a person sees, hears, or gets a knowing of something, it is best to not talk about it a lot, or, in some cases, to tell it at all, because you can literally blow the energy, and then the thing does not happen. If I see things I do not like, then, I talk about them and that blows the energy and they don't happen, but I am very careful about special things that I see and keep them quiet. I also write them down so that I may refer back to them later.

If you wish to further your development of clairvoyance, you may wish to develop your Seven Eyes. (Figure 7 shows their location. You may refer to page 127 of my book, *Kundalini and the Chakras* [Llewellyn Publications], for more information.)

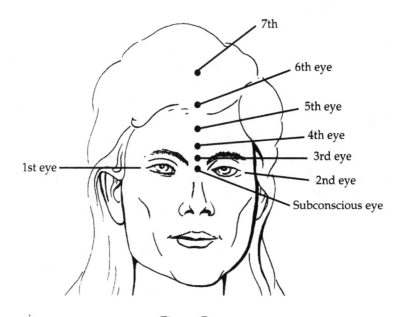

Figure 7
This figure shows the locations of the Seven Eyes and the Subconscious Eye.

VISUALIZATION

There are two forms of visualization. One is the practice of picturing in your mind something you want for yourself or for someone else. This sends the energy out into the universe to bring the particular item, quality, opportunity, or right persons to you or others.

The second form of visualization is to ask for a picture of what is already in the most probable future. You may also ask about possibilities available in a particular area.

Obviously, it seems wisest to ask what is the most probable future and then to use the first form of visualization to ensure the happening; or to use the first form to change the probable future, if you do not appreciate what you saw in it.

Every time we do a visualization, we plant a seed. Some seeds take longer to germinate than others. Some plants take a much longer time for maturity than others. You will find that some of the visualizations are answered immediately and others may take years.

Powers of visualization are increased many times if you can feel the visualization in your entire body and feel that you already have what you are picturing.

In order not to limit yourself to what your own mind can conceive, ask for what you want or to have something better. Keep in mind that God's will should come before yours.

Visualization is one of the strongest tools we have to shape our present and our future. It should be used wisely. Be sure you want what you visualize—you might get it. Visualization is a form of prayer which adds mental energy to the already powerful prayer energy. Prayer is the strongest form of energy (after love) available to us. Visualization added to our prayer energy makes it even more powerful. Enjoy it, but use it wisely. If in doubt, go to the top—ask God's guidance in your prayer visualization.

Meditation 1

If you are interested in your future, with the help of the energy from the center of your forehead you may ask to see what your probable futures are in a given area. (Some areas are blocked from our visionings for our own protection.) Then ask for a picture of what you can do in order to strengthen the force of the probable future you most wish for or feel is best for you. Then visualize this happening and feel it in your entire system.

Meditation 2

If you are in ill health or have a health problem, do not visualize the illness or problem. This only increases it. Instead, visualize yourself in perfect health and feel the visualization in your entire body.

Meditation 3

If you would like more prosperity, visualize yourself being prosperous, and enjoying it and using it wisely. Feel this in your entire body. To visualize only a specific way of becoming prosperous may block other opportunities.

Meditation 4

Do not visualize things for other persons unless they ask for your assistance. Otherwise, you are meddling in their lives. However, to visualize spiritual qualities for anyone can be a blessing for them and for you. Remember, the energy we send out for others comes back to us too.

Meditation 5

In the morning, ask for a picture of what your day is likely to bring to you. If there are things you do not like, ask for an understanding of them. Then use your visualization powers to help improve the probable future.

Meditation 6

Visualize a spiritual symbol above your head. It may be a cross, star of David, a thousand-petal lotus, or some other spiritual symbol. As you focus above your head you may feel it throughout your body, then ask if there is a message for you.

Meditation 7

Visualize Christ or some other spiritual personage above your head. Do the same as you did with the spiritual symbol.

CLAIRAUDIENCE

Some persons can hear so well that entire poems, articles, or even books may come in words as if being dictated. It would come as clearly into or from outside the person's head as if he or she was listening on the telephone. There may be a sense of not being connected to the voice or to the words; rather that they are coming from some other level. When they are your own thoughts, there is a sense of connectedness with them.

Hearing words psychically is very similar to a long-distance telephone call; you need to be somewhat focused but somewhat open. Sometimes there is the feeling of another person being in the room. You may even turn around to see who is there, only to find that you don't see anyone. Sometimes the person may hear conversations without seeing the people conversing. Sometimes it may be persons' voices that you recognize, or it may be persons you do not even know. You would just happen to be open to the frequency of hearing, as it would relate to the frequency from which they were speaking. You may even hear others talking about you and this can be disconcerting.

Celestial music has been heard by many persons and will be heard by many more in the future. It is indescribable and once a person has heard it, his or her life is changed. Sometimes composers or others will hear melodies or words, either in parts or in their entirety. This is not necessarily classed as celestial music. It can be very wonderful and very

---

Chart 3

SOUNDS AND PLANES

Physical Body:
  Lower—similar to thunder
  Higher—soft whistling like "whee"

Emotional (Astral) **Body:**
  Lower—roar of the ocean
  Higher—sound similar to gentle wind through the trees

Mental Body:
  Lower—bell sounds
  Higher—sound of waterfall or rushing water

Intuitional/Compassionate Body:
  Lower—similar to buzzing or light swarming of bees
  Higher—flute-like tone

Will/Spirit Body:
  Lower—wind
  Higher—humming, vibratory "OHM"

Soul Level Body:
  Lower—similar to violins carried by the wind
  Higher—reed sound similar to woodwinds (wide sound)

Divine Level Body:
  Lower—"Hu" (has a whispering quality)
  Higher—all sound, no sound, felt rather than heard

beautiful music, but celestial music is a much higher form. We really do not have the ability yet, as humans, to reproduce these sounds. There are sounds going on all of the time on our planet, and in the entire universe. Earth itself has a vibratory sound. All frequencies of energy have their own sound, their own color, their own sensation, their own musical tones, and combinations of these frequencies make for very beautiful vibratory patterns.

One of the most interesting phenomenon in clairaudience is hearing the sounds of our cosmos.

There are seven major planes which relate to our bodies. Each of these great planes is divided into an upper and lower level section. Below are these levels with their sounds. For the following exercise please refer to Chart 3.

Meditation 1

Focus on a particular level and imagine the corresponding sound as closely as you can. As you imagine that sound and feel it through your body, it will help you resonate with that plane. As you continue to practice this exercise, it will help some or all of these sounds to come in spontaneously. You will know it is not your imagination; it will have a transcending quality and you will be hearing the true sound.

THE SEVEN EARS

These ears relate to the bodies and planes just mentioned, as well as relating to the "seven eyes" previously discussed. (See figure 8 for locations.)

1st Ear, the right physical ear. If you are adverse to hearing about rules, regulations, or structure which affect you physically, you may have a tendency to shut off the right ear. This ear does help one to choose paths or forms

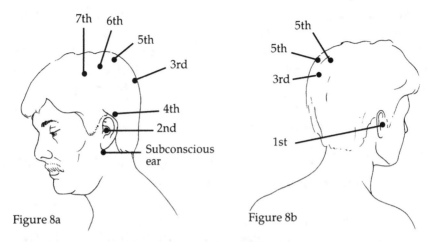

Figure 8a

Figure 8b

Figures 8a and 8b

These figures show the locations of the Seven Ears and the Subconscious Ears. Please note in Fig. 8a that the 1st Ear (the right ear), 4, 5, 6, 7 and Subconscious Ears have identical locations on the other side. Figure 8b shows another view of Ears 3 and 5.

which relate to the physical. It corresponds to the functions of the right eye.

2nd Ear, the left physical ear. This ear relates to the emotional body. If you don't wish to hear things of an emotional nature, you may have a tendency to block the hearing in the left ear. When you are meditating, focusing on this ear can help you relate to the emotional level or plane. This ear corresponds to the functions of the left eye.

You may enhance the psychic powers of the 1st and 2nd ears by focusing some energy just behind them, as well as in them.

3rd Ear, located in the center of the back of the head—the same location as the devotional chakra (see page 84 of *Kundalini and the Chakras* by this author). When open, this ear relates to the mental comprehension of higher truths, of really hearing in a more expansive way.

This ear has a strong relationship to the ego. Ego should never be squashed or held down. It has the function of caring for the physical, emotional, and mental levels. As a flower opens to the sunlight, so can the ego open to hear the wisdom of the one, true light. A closed ego has a difficult time of allowing spiritual truths in to help transform and regulate the human side of a person.

This ear corresponds to the functions of the 3rd eye.

4th Ears. These 4th ears are located off the edge of the ear between the top and back of the ear. These ears relate to the intuitional/compassionate level. These are strong observer ears which let you hear with greater compassion and understanding.

They correspond to the functions of the 4th eye.

The 5th, 6th, and 7th ears are in a line on the same level, just below the top of the head. It is the same area where many persons wear sweatbands around their heads.

5th Ears. These ears are located on either side of the back of the head. They relate to the will/spirit level and correspond to the functions of the 5th eye. They have to do with an even higher form of comprehension than the 3rd ear. The 5th ears relate to time, space, and the Akashic Records.

6th Ears. These ears relate to the soul level and are located just in front of the 5th ears. They help to hear spiritual truths which may sometimes come in ordinary conversations or in a very mundane situation. They correspond to the functions of the 6th eye.

7th Ears. They are located in front of the 6th ears, above the temples. These ears relate to the divine level and to the functions of the 7th eye. With these ears open, it is easier to discern what is right for you, to comprehend your path without stumbles or blocks.

Subconscious Ears

These ears are located just under the two physical ears, on the jaw. When persons close these off it is similar to "setting your jaw" and becoming inflexible. With these ears open your whole face is more alive, your jaw is more flexible, and you gain much strength from the subconscious levels to which they relate. The functions are similar to those of the subconscious eye. (See page 129, *Kundalini and the Chakras*, by this author.)

Meditation with Ears and Eyes

Using ears and eyes together greatly enhances meditations and can help open a person to greater consciousness. It is a very useful method to increase development.

The subconscious eye and ears are also used in this exercise as they help to open the person to his/her inner self. It also can help in understanding earth energy when the focus of the meditation involves nature.

The following meditation uses a tree for the focal point. However, you may wish to adapt this meditation to use other things for the focus as well. Nature, pictures, and mandalas are all appropriate for this type of meditation.

Meditation

Find a tree that allows for an easy visual access. Sit comfortably with your back erect. (Don't worry if you don't have an experience or receive a message each time. Be open for a time; if nothing comes, move to the next level. You may wish to refer to Figures 7 and 8a and 8b for locations of the ears and eyes.)

Sit loosely with awareness emanating from your subconscious eye and subconscious ears. Be aware of any messages coming in.

When meditating in higher levels, the senses have a tendency to meld or synthesize. This meditation is an excellent example of what can happen when sight and sound form a greater awareness.

After a few moments with this focus, go to the 1st ear (the right ear) and the 1st eye (the right eye). Repeat the directions as in the subconscious eye and ear.

Now do each level of the eye and ear(s) combinations.

Many persons fear developing clairaudience because of the possibility of hearing negative voices or misinterpreting messages. Some persons claim God has told them to do something negative. Actually, the message may have come from negative beings or negative thought forms. Also, a person is less liable to hear negative things or have his or her own thoughts turn negative when the psychic ears are more developed. This brings greater clarity and higher level insights.

No matter the source of the information, a person should always judge it in the light of reason. If it doesn't feel right, then it should not be acted upon. Since we are responsible for all our actions and inactions, we need to develop greater discernment.

CLAIRSENTIENCE

Clairsentience (clear sensing) is sometimes used to describe clear sensing; the ability to sense someone else's aches and pains. Clairsentience is a word that is sometimes used to cover all psychic or paranormal sensing, and sometimes it is used to describe only sensing through the feeling level. The latter description is what I will be using here.

This is the easiest and the most basic of these senses. Through this, one picks up others' aches and pains, others' moods, others' ways of being. Some persons are afraid to be in public because they pick up so much from other people. Sometimes it is easy to think that you are a hypochondriac when this happens. On the positive side, persons working with healing or energy changes in the body, or giving psychic readings, need this sense to be highly developed. Their bodies become sounding boards for what is going on with a particular client. This gives deeper insight into the other person. On the negative side, it can wear you out, it can be overwhelming, and a person can find himself/herself unable to do his or her own things.

The best protection from this is to fill yourself with the white light and strengthen your own vibrations.

Following are some meditations to help handle this:

Meditation for Protection

1. Fill yourself with white light and breathe into it. This helps to develop your energy pattern and strengthen it, so it is not so easily swayed by others. It also helps to develop your awareness of what is yours and what are other peoples' problems, concerns, or energies.

2. Stand in the middle of a room, take deep, peaceful breaths, and get the feeling that you are filling the entire room with your aura (energy force field around the body). This strengthens your energy patterns and your aura, so that you are more aware of other peoples' energies on the outside of your aura, and not inside your body.

3. Surround yourself with an ultraviolet light (you can't really see it, but your body does know what it is). This will let you know if it is someone else's energies that you are picking up or if it's your own. If it is someone else's, it fades away. If it is your own, it intensifies. Only hold the ultraviolet for a few moments. Any longer can block your own natural flow.

4. Exaggerate the questionable energy. If you become aware that it is someone else's, treat it as a call to prayer for that person. Pray that God be with them, that they receive their learning and release from the problem. Generally, it will leave your system upon recognition that it is not yours.

9

OTHER EXTRASENSORY PERCEPTIONS

A variety of things may happen during meditations. Following are some of the areas in which a person may experience paranormal happenings. These are the by-products of meditations and should not be considered the main reason for meditation. If a person becomes overly intent on the paranormal part of meditation, it will slow down growth. The overall growth and development of one's spiritual energies is the most important reason for meditating. Do not, however, block these paranormal or psychic experiences because they are a part of the growth.

Although the spiritual levels are of primary importance, we must also learn to function on all of the various levels and planes. As a baby is born with all of the tools to enable it to walk, talk, and otherwise function as a human being, needing only practice to accomplish them, so we also have the tools to enter higher levels and function as a spiritual being. We just need practice.

The following are some of the main paranormal experiences which may happen in meditation. Do not be frustrated if they do not happen in the beginning.

Knowing

Some persons get the feeling of *knowing* rather than seeing, hearing, or sensing. They know, and they know that they know, but they do not know *how* they know. It is a deep inner conviction, as though something had been written on their hearts or their minds. Usually with the knowing (as this type comes from a higher level of perception), a person does not question it as the sense of its reality comes with it. It can bring a deep, inner conviction to follow through with it.

Telepathy

Telepathy is the ability to read other people's thoughts, to know what goes on in their mental levels. If this happens to you, please respect the other person's privacy and keep things to yourself.

Sometimes it can be confusing to sort out which are your thoughts or which are another persons' thoughts. Surrounding yourself with the ultraviolet light for a few moments generally lets you know whose thoughts they are.

Thought Forms

Thought forms are masses of energy formed by strong mental activity. It forms a ball of energy, which then has its own life and its own volition. Its life span is determined by the clarity of the thoughts therein and by the power put into them. Some persons will have a number of these thought forms around their heads which may have been formed by day dreams, wishful thinking, anger, or focused thinking. Sometimes the thought forms will leave the person and hang around or become attached to the person who may have been the subject of the thought form (see figure 9). Many times a person will accept these thought forms as a part of their own thinking and modify their lives accordingly. These thought forms may be negative or positive. However, it doesn't matter if they are negative or positive, they still can interfere with that person's own thought process.

Figure 9
A person who is the recipient of others' thought forms which may interfere with his/her thought process.

If you feel that another person's thought form(s) is (are)
affecting you, you may imagine that you are surrounding
yourself with an ultraviolet light. If the thought form is from
someone else, it will disappear and you may have a
moment's awareness of the source. If the thought form is
yours, the strength of it will increase, which will then help
you work with it.

Some persons consciously send thought forms to others.
If you feel you are the recipient of these, you may send a
thought form message back telling the sender to discontinue
sending them to you. Another example is when a person goes
to do something and he or she can't remember what it was he
or she was going to do. He or she may have moved so quickly that he or she left the thought form in the location it was
first formed. If the person returns to the location where
he/she first had the thought, he or she can get in touch with
the thought form again and remember what it was he or she
was going to do.

Another example of this is when a person leaves a thought form of something to do near the task, and someone else comes along, picks up the thought form, and completes the task.

Thought Transference

Some persons' thoughts can be so clear and strong that it is relatively easy to transfer their thoughts directly to someone else without the use of spoken words. Animals are sometimes especially receptive to this form of communication.

Meditation

Put your attention on the center of your forehead. Let your thoughts or questions gently flow from that area to the equivalent in nature spirits or animals. Then let your forehead center be open, relaxed, and receptive to hear the answer.

You may wish to send your message by visualizing a symbol of your thoughts.

Subconscious Understanding

Subconscious understanding is when the person senses or feels what is in the other person's subconscious, whether it is deviousness, deep concern, fright, or other emotions. It relates to the emotional level and to deep, hidden things of the inner worlds. The other person actually may not be aware of these energies. The person with this subconscious understanding may doubt his or her own perceptions of it because many times the person perceived does not act based on that subconscious information.

Many people are so out of tune with their subconscious or ashamed of things if they are negative, that they really block this area and pretend it doesn't exist. Persons who pick up on the subconscious need to be very careful that they don't doubt themselves just because the other person doesn't follow through with what relates to that area. It is better to keep an open mind and a closed mouth on the subject.

Concepts

On occasion, a total concept of something will come through. It may take a half an hour to an hour or more to explain everything that came through in moments from a concept. If a person has a lot of this energy available, he or she would function from the conceptual mind.

Combinations

Occasionally a person may see and hear, sense and know, all at the same time. Obviously this is an excellent way. All of the senses are open and operating. It's similar to when you look at a beautiful meal, you enjoy the visual impact, the smell; sometimes you can almost feel and taste it. One of the reasons that eating is such a pleasure to many people is that it relates to so many senses at once, and includes emotions. It is as though the senses are operating together. When the higher senses are operating together, you may also get the feeling that something looks delicious and has no relationship to food, or something that you see feels tasty.

Sometimes injuries to the head or different areas of the body can increase perception. I do not recommend that type of thing—it is too dangerous. Patient developing of a person's energies, chakras, awareness, and willingness to be aware, are very important in opening up to these gifts. Generally, types of mental illness can increase abilities temporarily, but not usually in a manageable way. Persons with clairvoyance, clairaudience, and clairsentient abilities may or may not be highly developed spiritually, because this can be done through energy changes and other forms of work. It is best when there is spiritual development with it, as the gifts will remain longer. Spiritual development also brings greater understanding of what is experienced.

Essence

A very high level of awareness is to be able to sense the essence of other persons' ideas, beings in nature, spiritual beings, and so on. To have the essence of something is to know the nature of it—what it's about, what it's for, it's true inner nature. To understand the essence of a person is to know who he or she is, to know what he or she is about. This is difficult to do unless you are really in tune with your own essence—who are you really, what are you about? You can't really know yourself on a mental, descriptive level. When you want to fully know yourself, it has to happen on the essence level. This is a much higher form of perception than the others which are listed above, and is a higher form of intuition. Following are some meditations to develop this ability.

Meditation 1 — Your Essence

To discover your essence, sit quietly; let your mind be blank but let your spirit feel clear and strong. Let it move freely through you. This helps you to tune into your essence.

Meditation 2 — Essence in Nature

If you are interested in opening up to the deva kingdom—fairies, water spirits, and others—you may wish to be out in nature. It may be by water, in the woods, it doesn't matter, just so that it is someplace in nature where you can feel a magic sense, where the energy just feels magical. Sit quietly, tune into that energy, be aware of it. Feel the essence of that energy flowing over you. As you continue to do this and deepen your ability to perceive into this essence, you can then be aware of these beings, to see them, and even communicate with them by thought transference.

Divine

This is a very high spiritual level, very difficult to attain, very God-like. It is seeing or sensing as God does—to be divine. I am not indicating that we have the total ability to see and sense as the God force does, but we certainly do have some level of the God-like abilities within us, since we are created in the image of God and our whole being reaches toward enlightenment and oneness with our Creator. To divine you just know on very deep levels the patterns of things which exist and events that are coming. It is difficult to describe because it is so comprehensive and so pervasive. It is also very peaceful.

Meditation 1 — In Love with God

Feel yourself "in love" with God and filled with oneness. Let the pineal gland be open. Ask for information about something. Let a "knowing" flood your body.

Meditation 2 — Perfect Pattern of the Self

Tune into the "perfect pattern of the self," located behind the end of the breastbone. It is sometimes called the deep, still voice of the conscience.

Choose a thought or feeling about something on which you would like to have a "knowing." Hold that thought or feeling in the "perfect pattern of self" area. Breathe peacefully and deeply into it. Just be aware and let the "knowing" form.

Meditation 3 — Angels

Sit quietly. Raise your own vibrations to a high level. Ask to be aware of angels, to sense their essence. Feel love and light as you do this.

Psychic Smell

Psychic smell is sometimes included as a function of clairsentience. However, we are isolating it in this book because smell is such an integral part of our daily lives, and the psychic component of its ability is increasing in many persons.

Psychic smell can occur in a variety of ways. You can smell something from the past or something that is going on at the present time, but not where you are located; or you may smell a smell that is going to happen in the future. It is possible also through psychic smell to be aware of the very sweet aroma of angelic beings or very highly developed entities. Sometimes a person may be aware of his or her own "soul smell," or of the "soul smell" of others.

Meditation 1

Massage the sides of your nose. Breathe slowly into your nostrils, having the feeling that your breath is going into your forehead. Ask to remember: a favorite smell in your childhood home . . . a favorite smell outside when you were a child . . . a perfume or smell associated with a special happening . . . a smell that is important to you now.

Then ask: to be aware of a pleasant smell which is important to you in the future . . . to be aware of your soul smell . . . to be aware of the perfume of an enlightened guide or angel.

CLOSING

There are so many ways of receiving extrasensory perceptions that it is difficult to list them all. We are all like radio transmitters in that we are continually sending thoughts, feelings, or energy into the atmosphere. Some persons are stronger transmitters than others and some are able to direct it better and are much more conscious of it, but we all do transmit. We are also like receiving sets. We receive continually. Some persons have learned to close their auras so that they don't pick up as much, and most persons have, one way or another, closed their perceptual abilities so they do not pick up as much. It may have been through being emotionally hurt or not being able to understand the things that they have perceived.

As we grow and develop we are all called to live in a higher awareness. There is no way that a person can develop spiritually without developing these perceptions as well. They are part of the territory, they will happen. Each one has their practical application.

All persons, as mentioned above, have this potential and some have it much more than others. Certain persons will have abilities in one area and not the others, and as a person grows you will find these abilities will shift. You may have been very good in clairvoyance at one time, only to have the ability disappear. If that happens to you, let it go because your energies are shifting and you may now develop in clairaudience, clairsentience, telepathy, essence, or something else. Then the clairvoyance can come back at another time. When you are fully developed you will find that all these abilities are there, although there will be certain ones that will be your main strength. Some persons who have been active in the psychic field, doing readings and so on, will find that as they develop, their gift seems to disappear and they will start then to make it up or fake it, whereas, if they would just get out of the business for awhile, rest, and let other things develop, those abilities will come back again, usually much stronger.

I can and do caution you not to overdo the exercises. A slower, steady pace will help you develop faster than overdoing and having to quit for a time. I also realize that there will be those of you who do choose to overdo anyway. Physical exercise and sleep are two excellent ways to help recover.

You may find it rewarding to keep a journal of your experiences and insights. Many times a person sees things which aren't completely understood at the time and it can be very helpful to review the journal as your growth increases.

Chapters 8 and 9 give a very small portion of the information and experiences available with the development of the extrasensory perception. Whole areas have not been touched. Many of you will discover these other areas for yourselves. These sections are designed to give you some methods for opening these areas and to make you aware of the possibilities awaiting you in the total life.

10

OPENING TO NEW WORLDS

The energies of evolution are pushing us toward a greater understanding of the possibilities for mental and spiritual expansion, and it is becoming more apparent that we are not completed yet as human beings. During the 1990s this evolution seems to be accelerating, forcing us to find new ways to deal with the energies. Meditation is one of the best tools we have to make optimum use of this change.

Write down the areas in which you would like to grow, and those in which you would like to excel. Include steps for going about reaching those goals. Periodically make notes about your progress. Focusing in this way helps to form your intent, and that always speeds progress.

For many persons, relaxation and serenity are the beginning reasons for meditating and that is great. For others there will be a hunger to know more, understand more, and be more. The need to unlock the possibilities from other dimensions or worlds will become paramount in their quest. "Section II, Meditation Manual" of this book has exercises which will help in this area. *Kundalini and the Chakras* (by this author) can help open the evolutionary energy and make it more useable.

Meditation will soon let you become aware that there are many more things going on in the unseen world than there are in the world of sight. It has been said that earthly life is but a dream and the real living is on the other planes. Meditation is a way of opening up to this greater living while we are still in earthly bodies.

Meditation

Be in a meditative state, with your back straight and body relaxed. Let your breathing be peaceful and deep for a few minutes. Then take your attention from the breath. (The following type of meditation sometimes brings shallow and very quiet breathing to the meditator. This is fine as the body does not need as much breath during this state.)

Let energy radiate out all around your head, feel your energy going away from you, searching out information. Focus your consciousness on an imaginary spot anywhere from several feet to several miles away from your head. Let your consciousness be there.

Ask what information is available to you from that area. Be still and open. Let answers form in your consciousness. Then pick another area and do the same thing.

Variations

Do the exercise outdoors, focusing visually on a spot in the sky in the distance. Let the energy go deep inside you and do the exercise with the inner worlds. As the energy is loosely focused away from you, ask a particular question (should be clear and concise) and let your consciousness search out the answer.

Ask that your consciousness go to a particular spot on the Earth and ask what information is there for you. Ask that your consciousness go to another dimension and ask what information is there for you.

Do experiment with this type of meditative exercise—it will greatly expand your consciousness.

You may not understand all the information you get from these exercises. However, write them down and review them periodically. Sometimes understanding comes much later.

The expansion of consciousness is one of the greatest things happening to the human race at this time. Our seen world is certainly not the totality of life, and our journey into the unseen world has paramount importance at this time.

"For the things which are seen are temporal and the things which are not seen are eternal." (II Corinthians; 4–18 King James Version).

It is obvious that we are experiencing greater needs to explore and partake of the unseen areas in our lives.

SECTION II

MANUAL FOR EVOLUTION THROUGH MEDITATION

11

EVOLUTION THROUGH MEDITATION

Meditation expands consciousness so that new information is available and new ways of experiencing and
being become available. Persons become aware that there are
vast areas of knowledge waiting to be comprehended, and
great possibilities for development of paranormal abilities just
beyond their present grasp.

Understanding that there is much we don't know is the
beginning of real growth.

Meditation is a way of opening into these areas which
are beyond our normal thinking patterns. In fact, what we
now call "altered states" will be the normal consciousness of
the future. The consciousness or awareness achieved in peak
experiences will be more the norm.

Areas which we now call "unconscious" or "subconscious" will be fully available to us. We will find that these
areas are actually full of great information and wonderful
opportunities. There is nothing unconscious or subconscious
about these areas. It is we who are unaware. Most persons'
brains are not developed enough to comprehend these vast
areas. The levels of intuition are not sophisticated enough to
open the doors of insight into these greater realms.

There are among many persons a rejection of these areas. Much as most persons chose to see the world as "flat" in the past because they had no experience of its roundness, we, too, see our consciousness in a very narrow or flat way due to lack of experience. Reading of others' peak experiences and meditative openings do bring glimpses. However, it is the personal experience which will open the doors into these other realms. These experiences help us understand our misconceptions which hold back our development.

There are three main ways of opening up to the greater self:

1. Through the brain with its wonderful comprehending and processing ability;

2. Through the body and the development of awareness through experience; and

3. Through the development of the glandular system which plays a very important part in our growth as the glands are considered by many to be pathways to the spiritual or the more developed human.

Meditation is a vehicle for developing all of these areas and it will take time, patience, openness and practice. Meditation is truly a process for growth and not a religion itself, although it certainly can enhance or clarify one's beliefs.

It is important for each individual to search out the appropriate growth vehicles for personal use. The more information a person has available to him or her, the better informed are his or her choices.

12

MEDITATION AND COGNITION—THE BRAINS

A s we grow our brains must develop their ability to comprehend and process the information received. Expansion of energies is not that useful if awareness isn't developed. Experiences received through the body also need to be processed by the brains. It doesn't matter whether information comes to us through these experiences or intuition, insights, or visualizations, they all need to be processed by the brain.

As we progress in our evolution with our mental awareness or cognition, we can comprehend and process changes so that we can modify or enhance our practice for optimum growth. New levels or dimensions become a part of our consciousness. New skills are perceived.

We have different brain areas for different functions. Each needs its own development. The greater the collective development, the greater the synthesis of the brains.

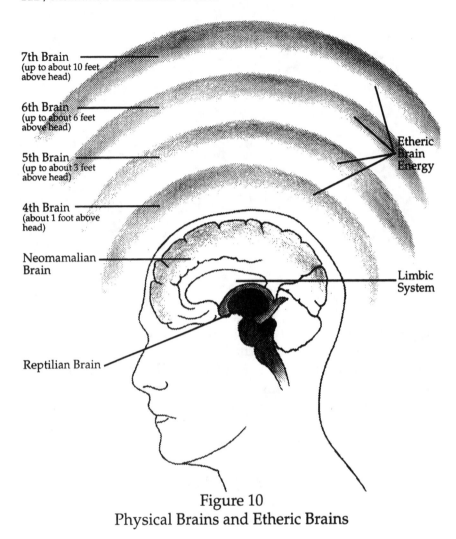

Figure 10
Physical Brains and Etheric Brains

THE BRAIN AREAS

Reptilian Brain (powered by primordial force)

Our first and most basic brain is the reptilian (see figure 10). It deals with territory, survival, and spatial perception. It relates to our physical body and is powered by the primordial force.

Meditation

Be aware of your reptilian brain inside the base of the skull. Send energy into the reptilian brain by imagining that you're breathing into it.

Survival: Does it have a good sense of survival on the physical level? The emotional, mental, and spiritual? (Meditate on each in turn.)

Territory: This has to do with the need for a person's own space, or a sense of belonging somewhere. Does the brain have a good sense of territory? Is space a problem for it?

It is especially difficult for children to learn if they don't have a particular sense of territory and survival, as it makes them overly watchful in these areas.

Spatial Perception: Do you have trouble staying in your lane when you're driving? Do you run into doors or walls? Is it difficult generally to comprehend the distances in the spaces around you? Be aware again of the reptilian brain and ask it what you can do to improve your spatial perception (just putting awareness in this area can generally be helpful).

The reptilian brain is powered by the primordial force (Earth energy). Good strength from this area helps in handling and balancing the emotional, mental, and spiritual energies. Ask to feel primordial force come into the reptilian brain to give it more strength and power. Then ask the reptilian brain in what instances in your life do you especially need to empower it more.

Ask the reptilian brain how it can help you in your growth.

Limbic System

The limbic system is powered by feelings and emotions. This second brain level is located between the reptilian and neo-mammalian brains. Its main functions are:

- Expression of self through feelings and emotions. Tune into your limbic system. Send it energy by imagining that you're breathing into it. Ask it which feelings or emotions are waiting to be expressed. Ask which ones are waiting to be developed.

- Sometimes we find ourselves expressing genetic feelings or emotions. Tune into the limbic system and ask what feelings or emotions that you express are not really yours but have genetic origins.

- Desire and motivation come from the limbic system and give us great energy for achieving things. Tune into your limbic system and ask where your desire and motivation are excessive. Ask in what areas of our life do they need to be further developed.

- When a person shuts off feelings or emotions it invites control from others. Tune into your limbic system and ask if you are doing this.

- Emotions are incredibly important in growth. Tune into the limbic system and ask how you can improve your growth and your world.

- Emotions are the beginning basis for spiritual development since spirit arises from feelings. Tune into the limbic system and ask if you are holding back your spiritual growth by not fully developing feelings. Then be aware of your limbic system and your feelings and emotions, and ask them to expand into joy and then spirit.

Neo-Mammalian

The neo-mammalian brain area is divided into two sections called right and left brains, and they are connected by a bridge called the *corpus collosum*. The left brain is related to the reptilian brain in function, however in a more expanded and highly developed form. Some of its purposes include perceptions, organization, and mathematics. The right brain is related to the limbic system but is much more expanded, and operates on thoughts as perceived by feelings. It relates to creativity.

Chart 4
BRAIN CHART

Brain	Location	Wave	Cycles per sec.	Function
Reptilian	Lower back of head	Beta	13–40	Spatial perception, ready for action, alert, extreme concentration, may be anxious
Limbic System	Covers over reptilian brain	Alpha	8–13	Calm, relaxed. May be euphoric
Neo-Mammal-ian	Right and left brains above limbic system	Theta	4–8	Creativity, problem solving. Meditative
4th Brain	Will be above neo-mammalian brain area when developed	Delta	0–4	For most persons this is a deep sleep area or unconscious space. As a person develops ability to handle energies, much information is available from higher spiritual and mental levels
5th, 6th, and 7th	Will be above preceding brain		Slower than Delta	Higher forms of healing, peak experiences, enlightenment

Right and left brains process differently. For instance, the left brain deals with the usual form of mathematics, the right brain function is numerology. Persons who have trouble comprehending math problems may wish to feel the numbers in the body and understand them from a feeling perspective first.

A person may play music which is technically very correct. This would be primarily using the left brain. Or, a person may play so totally from the right brain that there is great feeling and expression, but incorrect notes or other mistakes. The best is a balance of both brains with technical skill and with expression. Both brains deal with awareness and creativity but from their own special abilities.

Meditation

Think of a situation where you'd like to be more creative. Tune into your left brain by imagining that you are breathing into it, and ask the left brain how, from its energy, you can be more creative.

Then tune into your right brain and ask from its energy how you can be more creative in this situation.

Variations of this meditation are:
1. Asking a question about your growth and development.
2. How you can access higher mind to receive new insights.
3. You can ask where your problems come from in relationships.

Combining Right and Left Brains

The ultimate in the use of neo-mammalian brains is to balance right and left and use them simultaneously.

Meditation

Tune into your left brain and imagine you are breathing into it. Then tune into your right brain and imagine you're breathing into it. Then tune into the *corpus collosum* by imagining you're breathing into it. Feel all three areas as open, and right and left brains balanced. The *corpus collosum* should have from one-third to one-fourth the amount of energy the other brains do, otherwise you'll have a tendency to be spacey. As the brains are balanced, let some of the energy from the *corpus collosum* raise up and out the top of the head. This brings a balancing effect. It also includes some energy from the fourth brain. With this energy arrangement you may wish to re-ask some of the questions that you asked the brains individually in the meditation listed above.

Higher Brains

As we evolve more brains will develop. Each brain will relate to a particular vibratory rate (body level). (See page 176 for further information on body levels.) As we are coming into greater evolution, the 4th brain, still in the etheric stage, is now developing. It will take a long time to manifest in the physical. However, we can still use these areas for information and development. Some persons already have the etheric levels of brains 5, 6, and 7 somewhat developed. They are used in perceiving consciousness and healing. Peak experiences may occur when one of these brains is activated and greater awareness enters the person's cognition.

Meditation

Tune into the 4th brain by breathing into the top of your head and just above your head. Ask to feel the energy in the 4th brain. As you become aware of this energy, ask to know what expanded consciousness, healing or peak experiences you have had from this level.

Do the same meditation with 5th, 6th, and 7th brains, being aware that each one is further from the top of the head than the previous one. It's difficult to say the exact distance, but if you imagine that the 4th brain is about a foot above the head; the 5th is 3 feet; the 6th is 6 feet; the 7th about 10 feet above the head, it will give you a general idea.

Brain Wave Patterns

All of the brain waves generated by electricity from brain cells operate at the same time. However, one will be predominant and determine your functioning level.

You can learn to enhance a wave by concentrating on it and the area to which it relates. This helps to simulate brain development. See Chart 4.

Meditation

Be in tune with your reptilian brain and ask to feel the Beta waves at thirteen to forty cycles per second. Spend a few minutes here and focus on having heightened perceptiveness and sensitivity. Also try to feel a calmness with it.

Tune into a limbic system and feel the Alpha waves from eight to thirteen cycles/second. Feel your emotions as relaxed and peaceful.

Neo-Mammalian: Tune into your left and right brains. Ask to feel the Theta waves which vibrate at four to eight cycles/second. As the intensity slows down in the brain area, it should expand perceptive abilities. Insights can come in from here. Greater cognition and creativity will appear.

4th Brain: As you tune into the 4th brain be aware of the delta waves which vibrate from zero to four cycles/second. With this the consciousness is greatly expanded and it is very difficult to stay awake. If you can stay alert with this you will receive much information and see into other levels.

The 5th, 6th, and 7th brains do have their own wave patterns, but I do not know of any measurement of them at this time. With these levels it is very, very difficult to maintain consciousness and they are usually accessible only to those person with strong prayer or meditation practice.

5th Brain: Ask to feel the vibrations of the 5th brain. This is an excellent area from which to ascertain information about the galaxy and inner worlds.

6th Brain: Ask to feel the vibrations of the 6th brain. This is an excellent area to achieve contact with angels and higher spiritual guides, or one's own soul level.

7th Brain: Ask to feel the vibrations of the 7th brain. This is an excellent area to achieve oneness with your Creator and to comprehend the Divine in your life.

MEDITATIONS FOR GENERAL BRAIN DEVELOPMENT

Maintain Awareness

When you are meditating and you find it difficult to stay alert, take short breaths.

Retaining Memory of Meditation

Many persons comment that they have difficulty remembering the things that happen in meditations. Developing memory bridges to the higher levels such as the following meditation may be of some help:

Meditation

Feel your everyday awareness. Then expand and go into outer space. What do you perceive with your reptilian brain sense? What do you experience with your limbic awareness? What do you experience with your neo-mammalian awareness? Then bring the sense of that comprehension into the physical body. Let it go throughout the body.

As you do each step of the meditation, bring some of the awareness from each brain into your body and then feel it. Write down your perceptions, either when you get them or afterwards. If you still have trouble remembering, then you should write them down as you get them.

If you cannot conceive of something, then it is difficult to recognize or remember it. Reading other people's accounts of expanded awareness and peak experiences helps to give you a frame in which you can comprehend things.

You might also want to try being very open and then asking what new perceptions are there here for you.

Stilling the Brains

When we calm our busy brains, it allows higher mind to send information into our awareness.

Meditation

Have the feeling of floating so that you lift your awareness to a higher level. Let loose of your head and have the feeling the brain waves are settling into a relaxed pattern of receptivity. They don't have to push energy this way and that way to think of something or to plan something. By still and open for as long as it's comfortable. You may not get any new messages or information at the time, but with practice it will become easier.

Expanding Cognition

Since we are destined to function from higher levels it can be helpful to get acquainted with them and learn to function from there.

1. Ask to expand into a level that's new for you. Then be aware and see how it feels different.

2. Take some time to learn its properties. As you feel it, ask what its positive function is; what is its negative function; how should you use it? Does it have a name, so that you can contact it again?

Sideways

Use this to enhance meditations. When you are in a meditation and feel that you have about completed it, ask to go to the left of the meditation. What further information is there? Then ask to go to the right of the meditation space. What information is there? You may then follow it with asking it to go in front, behind, above, and below. This helps a person get into the fullness and greater meaning of the meditation area.

Brain Stem

Ask to be aware of the top of the brain stem. This is an area where Kundalini, as well as other energies, radiate into the brain. Visualize the area as open and clear, with good energy movement. You may ask the brain stem if there's something that you can do to facilitate this openness and clearness. This helps to vitalize the brains.

Meditation for the Evolving Brain

Our brain areas are still refining and developing. The following meditation can help in this process. You may wish to refer to chart 4 for the location of the brain areas.

Be in a restful, meditative state.

Be aware of your reptilian brain area. Ask to feel the beta waves flowing in that area. Give them a few moments to balance. Ask this area what you need in your environment. Ask what you need to help this area evolve.

Be aware of your limbic system. Ask to feel alpha waves flowing in that area. Give them a few moments to balance. Ask how your life would improve or change if you totally opened to your feelings. Ask what you need to help this area evolve.

Be aware of the neo-mammalian brain area (right and left hemispheres). Ask to feel the theta waves in that area. Give them a few moments to balance.

Let energies from the reptilian brain and limbic brain systems help to power the neo-mammalian area. What greater possibilities are there for you when you do this? Ask what you need to do to help this area evolve?

Be aware of the top of your head, the area of the 4th brain (still in the etheric stage—not yet manifested into bodily matter). Ask to feel delta waves flowing into it. Give them a few moments to center in.

Feel the peacefulness of this energy. Ask how you can learn to function better from here.

Ask what you need to do to help this area evolve?

Meditation—Balancing Brain Waves

Be in a comfortable position.

Be aware of the beta waves, then add awareness of the alpha waves, then awareness of the theta waves.

Let your head be opened and relaxed. Imagine you are breathing into your entire head, balancing all energies.

Spend a few minutes enjoying the restfulness and peacefulness. This aids in general healing and in overall development.

13

GROWTH THROUGH EXPERIENCE

E xperiences happen to us which alter our consciousness so
that it is difficult to maintain everyday reality. It makes it
difficult to function in the world. The ultimate goal in this
case is to be so expanded that we can maintain full awareness
in several or multiple levels, and function well in all areas.
This takes patience, training, and, above all, an openness to
new concepts.

Sometimes we consider the experiences as positives,
such as expanded awareness, ecstasy, spiritual oneness, or
great depth of feeling. Other experiences may seem negative,
such as depression, excessively strong sexual energies, or
heavy moods.

Past lives may spontaneously appear, or perhaps visions
of the future appear.

Whatever the unplanned experience is, we do need to
learn how to assimilate it into our lives and make it useable
for our growth.

Following are some areas of experiences which happen
to most persons. Meditators are especially more sensitive
to them.

SEXUALITY

Sexual energy is one of the strongest forces we need to learn to master. It alters our consciousness and our body functions. When it is flowing well it brings an aliveness to the entire system, including extra power and effectiveness. When it is blocked or does not flow well, it can slow down the entire system. It can turn a person to jelly or mush inside, make a person more assertive or forceful, or cause inappropriate or embarrassing behavior. Through meditation practice it can be transformed into other forms of energy.

Many persons choose to block the sexual energy, rather than learn to control or master it. However, blocking or repressing just doesn't work anymore. The increased astrological force we are experiencing is making it more difficult to block anything. Thoughts and feelings are more open, and that brings more energy for actions as well.

There is another possible problem with sexual energies. Meditation may increase the sexual energy because it helps in the release of any blocked energy and also increases spiritual energy. Since the sexual force is a lower octave of the spiritual force, the resonating of the new higher energy can trigger the lower octaves into greater action as well. It is then necessary to learn to transmute the excessive sexual energy into a more spiritual form.

Sometimes meditators may feel that God is testing their resolve by bringing extra sexual energies into their system. It is just the resonating of the higher octaves. It is more like the person is testing himself or herself.

Sometimes very spiritual persons do not have their human energies clear and balanced. This will tend to pull some of the spiritual energies down several octaves causing problems with sexuality or power. In some cases the person may encounter such difficulties in handling this energy in the lower octaves that the person may lose his or her marriage, career, or standing in the community through inappropriate actions.

It is very important to understand the implications of sexual energy beyond its usual use. Not recognizing and transforming or lifting up the energy can slow development. I do not believe a person has to be celibate in this day and age. Certainly there seems to be enough "voltage" of the energy for both levels. If a person tries to block sexual energy it will tend to block spiritual development as well. Following are some meditations to help in the handling of this powerful force.

Meditations

The following meditations move the sexual energy by thinking or imagining it where you want it to be.

When you have finished with any of the following meditations you may complete them by feeling that you are floating and being one with God.

Meditation 1 — Physical

Feel the sexual energy all over your body. Ask that its energy be doubled and turned into strength. Let the strength permeate your entire body.

Meditation 2 — Healing

Be aware of the superficial fascia (area just under the skin all over the body), let it be flooded with sexual energy. Breathe into it, feel the fascia being energized. You may then mentally direct this combination of sexual and fascial energy to any place in your body where you would like healing.

Meditation 3 — Emotional

Ask the sexual energy to mix with your feelings. Expand and enhance this combination through peaceful breathing. Let it transform into joy and spirit.

Meditation 4 — Mental

Bring the sexual energy to the lower back of the head to the reptilian brain area. Breathe into it. Let yourself have a greater sense of your physical body and its strength. This can help in greater feelings of self-worth and confidence.

Bring the sexual energy to the mid-brain (limbic system) in the middle of the head.
a. Breathe into it and allow a greater sensitivity to yourself and the world around you to come into your awareness.
b. Breathe into it and ask it to develop greater motivational powers.

Be aware of the right and left brains and the bridge between them (corpus collosum). Bring sexual energy into that area.
a. Breathe into it, let a greater sense of balance develop.
b. Breathe into it and ask for expanded creativity and productivity.

Meditation 5 — Spiritual

Let the sexual energy flood the superficial fascia (area under the skin).
a. Feel a sense of connectedness and oneness with your greater self.
b. Continue "a" and lift the sexual energy above your head; be open to oneness with God.
c. Continue "a" and "b". Also raise the sexual energy to a point above your head that is the same distance as your height. (If you are 5 feet tall, then the energy should go 5 feet above your head.) This puts you in touch with higher self and its greater powers. As you do this, feel that you are breathing into the fascia and the higher self areas. This can bring an awareness of tran-

scending your normal consciousness. If you wish, you may ask to be opened to a particular area in which you would like to be more "enlightened." Take time after the request to let answers or information form.

Some persons are so afraid of this sexual energy, through losing it or losing control of themselves through it, or just feeling that it is not okay to express it, that they will grow so far and then block further growth. This, however, does not work, since once you start your growth it seemingly has a force of its own and continues anyway.

Don't overdo the above meditations, as they can release more energy and blocks than is comfortable in handling.

ECSTASY AND DEPRESSION

These are definitely two altered states with which everyone is faced, especially the depression.

When a person feels depressed, the energy is "depressed into" the body. Depression comes from:

- Energy being depressed into the body (astrologically or psychologically) for getting in touch with inner levels and developing that level. Information, profoundness, strength, and healing are available from this area.

- A system that is not strong or healthy enough to have some of the energy flowing out of the body. It is as though the energy black holes into the system.

- It may happen to balance energy after a strong ecstasy or blissful state.

- There are also situations where a person's life is so shattered that the energy black holes itself. It is like "mind blowing" in the subconscious or feeling levels.

- Chemically induced depression.
- Chemical imbalances in the body.

Ecstasy happens when a person's energy expresses so far out around the body that higher, joyful states are reached. This can happen through:

- Adoration of the Divine.
- Meditation practice.
- Being "in love."
- Chemically induced.
- After-effect of depression—the energy bounces out of the system.

Following is a meditation to help balance depression and ecstasy. It also helps in losing the fear of these altered states.

You may wish to put the directions on tape or have someone guide you through the following meditation. It is best to be lying down for this meditation. Make sure you are not wearing any restrictive clothing.

Meditation

Feel like you are floating on water. Get a feeling of sinking deep in the water—no fear—no trouble breathing. Go deep—deep—down into the bottom. Feel totally free to go deep. Begin to slowly come up, gently and slowly, to the top of the water to the point where you are floating again. Then let yourself float into the sky—way up. Float on a cloud. Go beyond the cloud. Let yourself go way out with no problems breathing, etc. Now come back gently to the water so you are just floating on the water— totally open—totally free. Breathe beyond your hands, head, and feet. Let yourself be totally peaceful. You now know that you are capable of the depths and the heights.

Massage your navel so that it is relaxed. Start to pull the navel area energy deep into the body as though you are pulling it to the center of your being. Expand this inner level. If you are feeling depressed, the meditation is working.

Ask what is hidden in here? What idea? What fact?

Go even deeper inside. Is there a sadness in there from some interaction with yourself and others? Let it go deeper, deeper. Feel the pain and suffering of the world. What can you learn from it?

Tap into the collective unconscious. Bless it. Reverse the energy and let it come up until even with the body level. Let your energy go out—at least a mile. Feel the ecstasy state. Ask to feel the ecstasy and joy of the world (breathe out the sides of the chest).

Ask if there's a hidden message there for you? Is there a personal joy or ecstasy that you blocked out there?

Bring the energy back to the body. Get the feeling of integrating both heights and depths of feelings in your body. Let the energy diffuse throughout your body. Stretch and sit up.

You may do this meditation with the heart area (middle of the chest) and the top of the head.

Past, Present, and Future

If our consciousness was completely developed, we would have total recall of all our past lives and information concerning them, know all of the patterns manifesting in our current life, and be able to comprehend our probable futures. However, sometimes we can't remember what happened yesterday or what we are supposed to be doing today!

Meditation increases our consciousness and helps remove blocks on our awareness capabilities. Experiences from the past, deeper awareness of the current dynamics in life, and visions of our probable future begin to become recognizable.

It is a part of our evolution to develop greater awareness. This also means, however, greater responsibility in our actions.

In this lies a possible key to our unaware state. We tend to block what we don't want to deal with. If we block one thing we tend to block others. After awhile we feel lost and confused in life because so much information is blocked. Following is a meditation which may help to reverse the process.

Meditation

Let your body be totally relaxed. Relax your brains, feel them becoming calm. Have the feeling of floating. (This helps you to go past the blocked energy.) You may imagine you are floating on water or in the clouds.

Don't rush this meditation. Give time for answers to come to you.

1. Ask if there is a past-life experience or information ready to come to your consciousness.

2. Ask what else you need to know about your current life or your attitude toward it.

3. Ask what vision or information about the future is ready for you to acknowledge.

4. Meditate on what action you may need to take, or how your philosophy needs to change, as a result of the greater awareness.

Even if you don't receive any response to these questions the first time, it will still help to open your awareness, and information may come to you spontaneously another time.

BREATHING

Right breathing is an integral part of meditation. I prefer the deep, peaceful breathing which allows the body to make any adjustments it wants to. Do not try the intricate or powerful breathing meditations without a qualified teacher.

There are many interesting breathing techniques which a person can try. It can certainly enhance one's meditative level.

Meditation—Basic Breathing

Sit or lie down comfortably

Breathe in slowly and evenly to the count of eight

Hold the breath for the count of eight

Exhale for the count of eight

Hold for eight counts

Repeat.

You may start with a few minutes of this and then continue for longer periods as it proves valuable to you. You may also wish to time your eight counts to the rate of your pulse. Some persons like to use a shorter count such as six, or longer counts such as twelve.

You may wish to explore books or classes on breathing techniques. Do be aware that many times they release blocked emotions or thoughts, sometimes stronger than is easy to handle. An excellent book is *Science of Breath*, by Yogi Ramacharka.

PEAK EXPERIENCES

Most persons think of peak experiences as something which may happen, at best, only a few times in life. They are also thought to be spontaneous and cannot be induced. These experiences actually happen when a person touches higher energy (a higher "voltage") than they are used to. This releases information in the form of visions, either seen or felt or both, having tremendous experiences of transcendental states or other events which far surpass everyday existence.

It is possible, as a person develops higher awareness, to not only experience more of these peak happenings, but also to help bring them about by concentrated effort. However, later experiences may not have the "peak" feeling of earlier ones. That is generally because the person has developed an awareness closer to the level from which the first peak experience emanated. (See figures 11 and 12).

Some methods to opening to more awareness follow:

1. Concentrated prayer for at least three days on whatever a person chooses.

2. Fasting (I do not recommend this method as it can be too hard on the body). If you do this, please do it under the guidance of someone trained in this field.

3. Going on a vision quest that includes meditation time. This method is also best when under guidance.

4. If under great stress over something, take periods of time to expand into greater faith, patience, and awareness.

5. Taking time to reach the deep inner stillness, either through meditation or silent contemplation on a subject.

6. Focus on receiving greater awareness by balancing the same inner and outer level (See chapter 17, preferably levels 4 through 7) and expanding the energy. It helps if you have a question or ask for a quality such as patience, love, joy, etc.

It seems to me that most peak experiences come when there is great balance and expansion of combined inner and outer levels. That type of meditation can open doors to greater knowledge, qualities of being, and awareness.

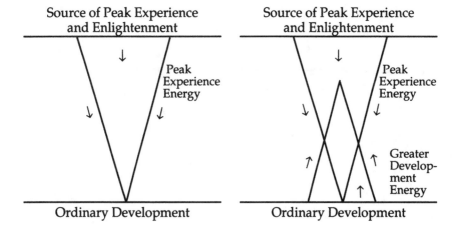

Figure 11
Early Peak Experience is very strong.

Figure 12
Later Peak Experience seems more normal since the person is more developed.

ENLIGHTENMENT

There are many levels of enlightenment and it reaches into many areas. It basically means the light is on something and you understand it. You can ask for enlightenment in certain areas, but I would qualify it with asking that it comes in a peaceful manner. No need to go through great struggles and pain to learn if we don't have to. There are easier ways to learn, but it involves being aware and paying attention when it is time to experience something new or to open to new possibilities or understandings.

Many persons are afraid of enlightenment or spiritual growth. They may feel that they are not worthy or may have to change. There is always the possibility of being more responsible! There are always changes involved as we grow. However, it can enhance where we are and what we are doing. Whatever a person has to go through to reach the higher levels is usually well worth it.

14

GLANDS

GLANDS AND GROWTH

G lands have definite and important functions in the maintenance and well-being of our bodies. However, they are also gateways to higher vibrations and are very important for balanced growth. Although we think of kundalini and spiritual energy as very strong energies affecting growth, the glandular energy is important as well.

Developing the glands allows better energy to flow through the chakras. Likewise, good chakra flow enhances glandular functions. Any aberration in either affects the other.

It is important to open to the higher function of the glands, and it is especially important that the glands be reasonably balanced in their openness and useability. This gives a more centered approach to life, and a person is able to have better control of his or her emotions and thoughts. It also helps in the general well-being and in the health of the body.

You will note that there are some glands included which are not usually listed (see figures 13, 14, and 15, and chart 5).

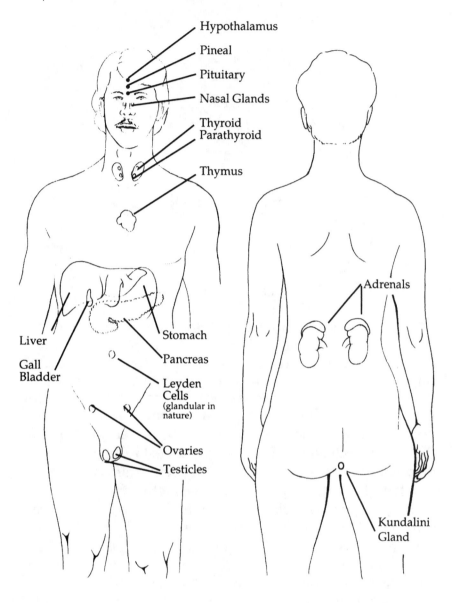

Figure 13
Front

Figure 14
Back

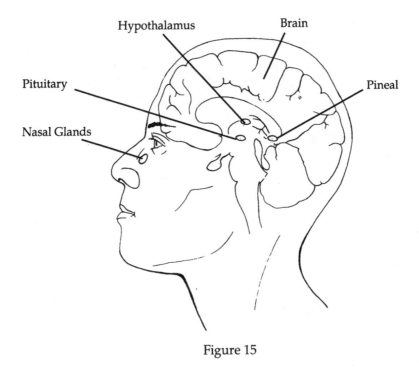

Figure 15

Unusual Glands

Kundalini Gland

There is no medical or scientific basis to corroborate the existence of this gland at this time. It is the opinion of this author that the Kundalini gland does exist—however, not in most persons in the physical level. It is similar to the higher brains which are operating on the other levels, but haven't manifested in the physical body. It is believed by this author that persons who have Kundalini awakenings have begun development of this gland, and that in the future most persons will have it active in their systems.

Some persons may choose not to work with the Kundalini gland for fear of it. Many release too much of the evolutionary energy. Consult my book, *Kundalini and the Chakras*, for further information.

This gland is located between the anus and the genitals.

Leyden Cells

Edgar Cayce refers to this area in some of his writings. J. Everett Irion talks extensively of this area, which is glandular in nature, in his book, *Interpreting the Revelation with Edgar Cayce*. Irion reports that Cayce calls the leyden cells the center of the spiritual forces. It is this author's belief that through this area the Ki or Chi flows; that it also is the point of entry into the energy of the collective unconscious. The energy of the collective unconscious can bring incredible spiritual, or very negative, almost diabolical, force.

Nasal Glands

These are newly discovered by Johns Hopkins investigators. These glands are located on either side of the nose (see figure 15).

These newer glands are included because of their importance in our overall growth.

Meditations for Glands

Following are some meditations for the development and use of the glands. (Please refer to chart 5 for information on the glands.) You may wish to do several glands at a time. Working with the glands does activate them. There are eighteen listed and, if possible, try to do all within a week. Taking a longer time will leave you unbalanced.

If you run into problems with the energy released becoming too buzzy or heavy, stop and balance the systems by lightly being aware of each of them. Positive results are healthier bodies, more integrated systems, and greater openness to higher levels.

You may feel exhausted or heavy after the first time you work with the glands. This is normal. If heaviness persists, walking or gentle movement usually lightens the energy.

Occasionally you may feel hot flashes as the glands are balancing.

If something seems out of order, do see your doctor.

Meditation 1 — Awakening Glands

Be in a meditative state. Be aware of each gland in turn beginning with the Kundalini gland. (If it seems too buzzy don't spend more than a moment there so as not to stir up too much energy.)

Ask each gland to function gently and correctly.

Breathe deeply and peacefully while concentrating on each gland. Letting your thoughts and feelings emerge can bring information locked in a gland. It is good to release the energy of the thoughts and feelings as they can hamper proper functioning.

Remember, you don't have to finish all of them at once.

Meditation 2 — Glands and Functions

Be in a meditative state, preferably lying down. Refer to chart 5 and meditate on the functions of all three levels of each gland. (Use the positive on the emotional/mental level).

Be aware of the physical functions during one meditation and at other times use the emotional/mental or spiritual functions.

Meditation 3 — Balancing through Colors

If you go slowly you may find you receive information which affects the particular gland.

You may wish to do only three or four glands at a time as it is difficult to keep the concentration in the beginning. Again, do try to finish the entire system within a few days—preferably the same day.

This meditation is very time-consuming, but an excellent one for balance, healing, energizing, and uplifting the glands.

Concentrate on each gland, in turn, beginning with the sexual gland. (It is best not to use this with the

Kundalini gland as it may arouse extra Kundalini before your system is prepared.)

Fill each gland with the rainbow colors in this sequence: Red, Orange, Yellow, Green, Blue, Purple, and end in Radiant White

Meditation 4 — Developing through Glandular Energy

Be aware of each gland in turn and meditate for a few minutes on the information given for the gland. You may wish to write down the information you receive.

Gland Development

Kundalini: Ask to feel what evolutionary potential is opening for you from here?

Ovaries or Testicles: In what areas is your sexual energy searching for polarity balancing (besides its usual use)?

Leyden: What power from the past wants to emerge from here? What spiritual discernment wants to come to your consciousness?

Liver: Feel the liver. Let it send strength to your heart. What is it trying to tell you is spiritually right for you?

Gall Bladder: Let it give you good feelings about yourself. Let the good feelings spread all over your body.

Stomach: What changes in your life have been difficult to accept—to "stomach"?

Adrenals: What messages of appropriateness in your life are trying to come from here?

Thymus: Love is like a cosmic glue which strengthens this gland. Ask in what situations you have too much "cosmic glue" and in which ones don't you have enough?

Thyroid: What, besides food, would this gland like to accept and use?

Parathyroids: Do you have some rigid beliefs these glands would like to lighten up?

Nasal: Let it balance the power of heaven and earth in your system.

Pituitary: Do you feel or see your visions? Ask this gland how to improve this ability.

Pineal: Feel Divine Light pour into your system.

Hypothalamus: What earthly concerns block your heavenly visions?

Brain: How would it like to regulate your system better?

Lymph System: Is your garbage primarily physical, emotional, or mental? How can you help it do its job better?

Skin: What messages does it have for you?

Meditation 5 — Pineal and Pituitary

When these two glands are well-developed on all levels, a golden glow emanates from both of them, giving the appearance of being one. This helps in achieving higher states of consciousness.

Be aware of the pituitary gland on all three levels— physical, emotional/mental, and spiritual, releasing any unwanted attitudes, feelings, or tensions.

Do the same with the pineal gland.

Then become aware of the pituitary and pineal being connected with a golden glow. Let this energy radiate over the top of the head. Feel yourself as floating and opening to greater awareness (consciousness).

Follow by being in an open state, letting insights enter your awareness.

Meditation 6 — Transformation of Sexual Energy to the Pineal Gland

Ask your sexual energy to either:
1. Radiate up through your body into the pineal gland, or;
2. To enter the spine, traveling up through it and at the brain stem moving into the pineal gland.

If you cannot see or visualize this, then imagine the energy as following your instructions.

When it reaches the pineal gland, you may:
1. Radiate it out to the entire brain to help it develop, or;
2. Let it go out the top of the head about 10 feet and rest in peacefulness, or;
3. Spread it out from the pineal gland beyond the entire body. This helps to develop awareness.

A few minutes is long enough in the beginning as this can be a very powerful meditation.

Meditation 6 — Thyroid and Parathyroid

Focus attention on your thyroid. How well do you accept your growth potential? Expand into awareness of the parathyroid as well. Have faith in the evolutionary process and your part in it.

Meditation 7 — Hypothalamus and Visions

Focus attention on your hypothalamus. Let energy from it flow through your 6th eye (below the hairline, directly above the 3rd eye). Let the energy flow from there away from your head until the energy feels light and transformed. Be still and be aware of feelings or pictures. A feeling of oneness may arise or visions may appear.

CHART 5

Gland	Chakra	Physical Level	Emotional/Mental Level	Spiritual Level
Kundalini	Base	Secretes electrical-like energy—rejuvenates cells and cleanses blocks.	Pos.—Refines and evolves emotional and mental energy. Neg.—Can cause aberrations and illness.	Opens to higher spiritual energy—raises consciousness.
Gonads, ovaries and testicles	Sex	Secretes hormones that balance pituitary and thyroid. Controls hormonal function.	Pos.—Polarity balancing with others. Power, charisma, playfulness. Neg.—Sexual obsession.	Transmutes to spiritual energy.
Leyden Cells (Has glandular action)	Solar plexus, navel, (just under the navel) and 3 sex chakras	Feel life in self.	Pos.—Brings order, clarity. Neg.—Disorder, confusion.	Opens to spiritual forces from inner worlds—tumo or spiritual heat.
Liver	Liver Chakras	Detoxifies, helps digestion. Produces red blood cells.	Pos.—Acting on spiritual beliefs, courage. Neg.—Fears, depression, blocked.	Opens to spiritual direction, full of life
Gall bladder	Right companion chakra to solar plexus	Aids digestion, especially fats.	Pos.—Embraces life. Neg.—Anger, defiance, depression.	Understands bigger picture of life. Recognizes others need space.
Pancreas	Solar plexus	Aids digestion, regulates carbohydrate metabolism.	Pos.—Opens to sweetness of life, joy. Neg.—Won't accept good things for the self.	Brings spiritual energies into everyday life. Empowers a person's sense of destiny.

CHART 5 (CONT'D)

Gland	Chakra	Physical Level	Emotional/Mental Level	Spiritual Level
Stomach (Cardiac, fundic, pyloric glands)	Left companion chakra of solar plexus	Digests food.	Pos.—Digests emotional and mental energy to aid in nourishment. Neg.—Blocks all digestion.	Sorts out what is helpful for systems.
Adrenal	Adrenal chakras	Increase blood pressure, liberates glucose from liver, regulates water and electrolytes.	Pos.—Courage for action. Neg.—Excessive anger or depression Fight or flight.	Opens up to greater abilities to function. Brings great strength.
Thymus	Compassionate heart chakras	Works with the immune system.	Pos.—Loving, immune to negative influences. Neg.—Can't function and protect the system.	Brings in higher forms of love and healing.
Thyroid	Throat chakra	Governs metabolism.	Pos.—Accepting, processing. Neg.—Not accepting,processing, prideful.	Creative in life. Accepting of higher purpose in life.
Parathyroids	Throat chakra	Regulate blood/calcium levels. Works with nerves and muscles.	Pos.—Living from faith. Neg.—Living in fear.	Trust and faith in universal principles.
Nasal	Power nose chakras	Warns of negative things through smells. Induces appetite.	Pos.—Enhances life. Neg.—Rejecting.	Opens to higher consciousness, through some smells bringing an awareness of God. Balances power of heaven and earth.

144

CHART 5 (CONT'D)

Gland	Chakra	Physical Level	Emotional/Mental Level	Spiritual Level
Pituitary	3rd and 5th eyes	Controls water absorption, blood pressure, slows.	Pos.—Psychic sight, visionary. Neg.—Narrow minded.	Opens to spiritual and high mental possibilities. Brings expansiveness.
Pineal	4th and 7th eyes	Stimulates the adrenal cortex.	Pos.—Balance personality/spirituality Neg.—Closed minded.	Doorway to God and God Consciousness.
Hypothalamus	6th eye	Body regulator, maintains balance.	Initiates fight or flight response that goes to the Kidneys. Pos.—Deals with basic pleasure and well-being. Neg.—Can release excessively angry feelings.	Helps in development of intuitional brain. Opens to oneness with all.
Brain		Master computer.	Pos.—Ability to function. Neg.—Inability to function well.	Comprehends higher mental and spiritual information.
Lymph System		Cleans garbage from system.	Pos.—Flexibility of thoughts and feelings. Neg.—Rigidity, negativity, fear.	Purification; holiness.
Skin		Protective agent, controls temperature, and excretes toxins.	Pos.—Enhances relating to others, warns of negative energies. Neg.—Closes off to others.	Receives information from vibrations.

(Note: For further information on the chakras, please refer to *Kundalini and the Chakras* by Genevieve Lewis Paulson, [Llewellyn Publications].)

15

MEDITATION AND EVOLUTION

SPEEDING EVOLUTION

Not only does meditation alter our consciousness, it gives us more flexibility in our actions and reactions, and also makes us aware of more choices. We become more alert and recognize our greater potential. It is one of the great benefits from this practice. It helps us be more of who we can be, by expanding us from our normal levels of awareness. This type of expansion speeds our evolution. As we progress in our growth, our consciousness shifts (see figures 16 and 17).

3 - Superconscious	3 - Superconscious
———————————	↑ ↑ ↑
2 - Normal Consciousness	2 - Normal Consciousness
———————————	↓ ↓ ↓
1 - Subconscious	1 - Subconscious

Figure 16
Limited range is held in 2nd or normal waking consciousness.

Figure 17
The more developed person has no barriers and has access to both subconscious and superconscious levels.

Unlimited Possibilities
by Ruth Allen

We are so much more than physical form. There are no limits to the mind and soul except those imposed by the body. Our fear of failure and discomfort keep us locked into using and protecting our bodies, and this fear imposes imagined limitations on the mind and soul. We tend to measure the mind and soul with the yardstick of the body. It is like comparing apples with the wind.

We need to get in touch with our limitlessness, to know that we are more than muscle and bone. We need to know, that we do, indeed, go to the edge of the universe. Not only do we fill the universe, but the universe fills us. We need to carry with us the dual awareness of our spirituality and our physicality, and to be a particular one while being a part of a greater One.

The following meditation is designed to put you in touch with a greatly expanded Self while keeping you grounded in your physical body. It is not an out-of-body experience, although awareness of the body may fade. We are body, mind, and spirit, a tripod with each leg equally strong and straight. Our bliss, to be truly evolutionary, must be manifested through the physical form. That is the reason for our incarnation.

Meditation

Sit with spine erect or lie flat so the spine is straight. Relax and begin to breathe slowly and deeply without any pause between the inhalation and the exhalation. As the body settles into a comfortable position, become aware of the rhythm of the breath.

---

* Printed with permission. Ruth Allen, Orbis, Louisville, KY.

Feel the sides of the body expand and contract. Mentally say to yourself, "Expand" as you inhale and "Relax" as you exhale. Let the body be comfortable and the mind still. Then become aware of the front and back of the body as well as the sides, as you breathe in and out, expanding and relaxing. Continue breathing like this for two or three minutes.

As you inhale and expand, keep your awareness on that space all around your torso where the expansion of your body ended and keep focused on that expanded space, even as you exhale. Keep the breath flowing evenly in and out. When your awareness is focused on the outer limits of the inhale, then let awareness spread out six inches away from the body, then eighteen inches; six feet; twelve feet. Keep expanding beyond the body. You are both in your body and beyond your body.

As you fill the space around you, feel the vastness, the infinite, the eternal. There are no walls, no barriers, no limitations. It is awesome, and, perhaps, a bit scary. But you are firmly anchored to the earth by your body, and you continue to breathe deeply into the space. Stay with this awareness for four or five minutes, or as long as you can.

Let the envelope of your skin become porous so that the spaciousness can permeate to the core of your physical being. Feel it in your head and in your spine, down into your arms and legs—totally beyond time and space, but also in the here and now.

When you are ready, begin to move gently and to stretch, and sit quietly for a few moments to absorb your feelings and sensations.

MIND BLOWING

The phrase "it blew my mind" is used many times by persons to describe something which has happened that their minds cannot comprehend or process. The person's consciousness (cognition and awareness) is ineffectual in dealing with the expanded energy entering the brain.

This happens in meditation as well. The person cannot describe what has happened to him or her, or there is no memory of the meditation afterwards.

It is important to learn to expand our consciousness so that comprehension can be made of the strong, expanded, or very high energies. Since evolution expands our potential and brings greater development we need to train our consciousness to function better. The following meditations will help in awareness of this problem and of development.

Meditation 1

Expand energy out several feet around your head. Breathe into the top part of your lungs (this opens higher consciousness).

Put your consciousness (awareness, cognition) into that energy. What is happening around your head? Take time for the information to form in your consciousness.

Breathe into all of your lungs so that the information permeates all of your body.

Meditation 2

Think of a situation which has happened recently which "blew your mind." Open to it, breathe in the top of the lungs. Expand your consciousness above your head. What thoughts come through?

Breathe through your entire lungs. How does your body "read" the event?

Some situations are meant to be felt as well as comprehended mentally. Sometimes it takes a whole body reaction to process effectively.

Meditation 3

When having trouble comprehending someone, open the center of your forehead and let energy flow gently out. This will offset any overpowering energy being directed at you by the other person that might be blocking your comprehension.

Meditation 4

With the push in growth it can be helpful if you practice letting your consciousness expand more naturally.

Expand consciousness around your entire system (head and body) every day for a few minutes. Then be aware of how this changes your approach to life.

BABES ON HIGHER LEVELS

As a baby needs to learn to walk, talk, and function with his or her new body, so do we need to learn to "walk, talk, and function" on higher levels or octaves of energy. It isn't enough to achieve higher levels in the meditative state. We are called to be able to be aware and effective on those levels.

Meditation

Through whatever meditation style you prefer, let yourself be raised to higher vibrations, or you may prefer to have the feeling of floating in space.

Really be aware when you have reached a different vibratory level.

Practice functioning there by asking questions about the level you are on, its functions, positive and negative uses, what it means in your life, or any other questions which come to your mind.

Ask the level if it has a name or some other way to identify, it so that you can contact it more easily in the future.

Write your information down—this will help you "map" your higher levels. Then you may ask to go to another level and repeat the sequence.

It is important to learn to talk to consciousness. All vibrations have consciousness and it is possible to have dialogues with them.

Meditation is a vehicle for accelerated growth. It definitely speeds up the process of your evolution. It sometimes speeds up your cleansing as well. Usually that is not quite as difficult as it sounds, because the meditator has learned skills with which to work on troubling situations. Also, a long-time meditator is usually ready for stronger experiences. If you are still having trouble with excessive cleansing you may wish to limit your meditations for awhile.

There are several ways in which a person can change a meditation in order to get more "grit" from it. The same technique is useful in working on problems. Below is information which can be used for both areas.

Empowering Your Meditations

1. Choose a meditation with which to work.

2. As you approach the meditation in the regular way, ask that the energies go deeper, or higher.

3. Ask the universal significance of the meditation.

4. Ask how it can empower your growth in further ways.

5. Have the feeling of going off to the left of the meditation energy—what information is there? Then go to the right of the meditation energy—what information is there?

6. Combine meditations—for instance, use different colors as background energy for a different meditation. Or you can do the same meditation from different body levels to see what information you can get.

Problem Solving through Meditation

1. Concentrate on the situation, then let the energy go and be in an open meditation and let information come to you.

2. You can then ask specifically, if this is karmic and does it need to be balanced? What am I to learn or do about the situation?

3. If it is a growth opportunity in order to learn new skills, then ask what new skill or understanding is available to learn.

4. We go through various tests in our growth as we achieve certain evolutionary levels. You can also ask if the situation is a test and how can you pass it?

5. Ask what the universal purpose of the situation is. Is there something greater going on that involves much more than just your world? Ask how you can help.

PRAYER AND MEDITATION

Prayer lives are enhanced by the practice of being in meditation states before and/or after the prayer. The meditation helps a person tune into deeper levels and be more aware of what is being prayed about. It is easier to recognize answers when they come as well.

Combining prayer and meditation also helps to develop intuition and helps to put the person into a level where they feel led to do the right thing at the right time and opportunities come when needed. A person feels truly led along his or her own path.

As a person advances, meditations will begin spontaneously in the person's system. Do let it happen. Watch, observe, ask questions of the energy if you wish, but primarily let it alone. It will have its own agenda (which is for your growth) and its own methods. It can be very helpful to write the event down afterwards so that you can repeat it if you wish. When a number of these happen, you will begin to see the pattern of how your higher self is guiding your growth.

16

ALTERED BODY STATES

As meditative abilities develop, it is possible to alter body states consciously. Although out-of-body-experiences, trance states, levitation or other altered body states may occur spontaneously, if a person is knowledgable about this phenomenon, it isn't so frightening and can be worked with better.

TRANCE

Trance is a state where normal consciousness is not operating. There are two types of trances. One is where the person goes into a trance-like or hypnotic state. This is usually caused by a person achieving much higher levels then normal and the memory bridge is not developed nor are perceptive abilities developed. It can be incredibly healing, inspiring, and can be considered a peak experience, even though no cognitive experience is remembered.

Another form of trance is where the person not only is not aware, but allows another entity to speak through his or her body. Sometimes the entities are of a very high level and very wonderful information can be received. Edgar Cayce was certainly an example of this. If you are interested in further developing this, do find a competent teacher to help you. Then you will be able to get the most from it.

On the negative side, there may be a possibility of lower entities working through the person. This can be averted by a person's understanding of the process and their taking precautions to get connected with higher levels.

If you feel you are going into a trance and don't wish to, breathe rapidly and deeply, as though "huffing and puffing," for a minute or so. Walk around, get fresh air, and concentrate on your physical body.

DUAL AWARENESS

Meditation — Twilight Zone

This meditation quiets the body and allows the mind to become very clear.

Let the body be totally relaxed, almost as if in sleep. Breathing from the very top of your lungs, ask prana (life force that is strong in the breath) to enter the brain area. Focus consciousness in the brain. Let your body be totally relaxed and your mind totally alert.

If you can stay in this dual awareness for five to ten minutes you will feel very refreshed. Sometimes pictures will appear or information will come to your consciousness.

Meditation — Gravity of Earth and the Heavens

In a relaxed position, feel yourself pulled by Earth gravity until you feel very heavy and thick.

Let go of Earth gravity and ask to feel the pull of heavenly gravity until you are light and free. A sense of floating helps.

Ask to feel both earthly and heavenly gravity at the same time—heavy and light.

Feeling the dual awareness of both heavy and light is excellent as a preparation for seeing past lives. It is also a way of balancing energies.

LEVITATION

Levitation is the raising of the body without external aid. A person may float, walk in the air, or walk on water. These are not your typical responses to meditation. However, they do happen.

There are a number of reasons to practice levitation, including the following benefits:

- Levitation promotes lightness, openness of the body.

- It clears the mind.

- It aids in general well-being.

- Physical movements are easier.

- You will feel less bound by time and space.

- It helps to release emotional and mental blocks.

- It makes you more open to spiritual dimensions.

Following are some meditations which will help in the development of the above listed benefits, even if you don't get off the ground. If you do levitate, tell yourself to land softly.

Meditation 1

Totally relax the body and clear the mind. Focus on energy up in the air where you would like to be. You may see it as an intense orange. Become one with the energy.

Meditation 2

Open the center of the chest (between breasts). Concentrate on its energy. Think of where you would like to be. Let the energy of the focus on the chest be one with where you would like to be.

Meditation 3

Open the sides of your chest, feel that you are breathing through them. Feel like you are floating and filled with ecstasy. Be one with the heavens.

Meditation 4

Fill your physical body with the color of light blue and experience a floating feeling. Fill your etheric body (a lighter part of the physical body) with brilliant orange.

Feel yourself one with the vibration of space and able to move around in it under control of your thought power.

OUT-OF-BODY EXPERIENCES

Out-of-body travel, sometimes referred to as astral projection or soul travel, is a means by which our consciousness leaves the physical body and its limitations. Our consciousness is then not under the restrictions of time or space, and in just moments may move halfway around the world or into outer space, exploring and observing. As we get further into the Aquarian Age, with its increased energies, more people are doing this type of travel in full consciousness, some with joy, and others with fear. Although everyone has some out-of-body travel while asleep, it is relatively unusual in full consciousness.

There is some disagreement among authors and other experts as to what out-of-body experiences really are. It is becoming increasingly clear that there are several forms of such experiences. I shall divide them into three categories: astral-, mental-, and soul-level travel. Each of these has a different quality, different purpose, and different ranges.

Astral Travel

First, we will look at astral travel, probably the most commonly known and widely experienced. During astral travel the consciousness is in the astral (emotional) body or level of energy, and can leave the physical, either by itself, or with the mental and soul level energies. The sense of still being in the physical body is quite strong. However, the consciousness remains in the astral level. Characteristic of this type of travel is increased awareness of sounds and feelings. Intense fear or intense excitement may be felt. Astral sight, a different form of seeing, causes objects to appear to have a whitish outline and be not quite as clear as when viewed with physical sight. A person may be able to see from all sides of the "body."

When traveling in the astral body, it is possible to travel through intensely negative areas, areas which can only be described as hell. These areas are also known as lower astral levels, where the most negative and depraved human emotions are found. In the highest astral levels, a heaven-like region may be found. It is one of the lower-heaven levels.

Sometimes one may visit not only with persons who are living, but also with persons who have died. Many persons have friendships on these other dimensions, regularly visiting and sharing experiences. If this occurs in the dream state, then the everyday consciousness usually knows nothing of these relationships. However, sometimes a person may meet an out-of-body experience friend and instantly feel a close friendship. This may, of course, be caused by a past-life experience or a similarity in energy patterns, but quite often it is the result of a friendship developed during the dream level out-of-body travel. Sometimes the persons may actually have arranged to meet at a certain place—to "run into one another" and "get acquainted" on the physical dimension.

The navel is the usual area for the astral traveler's exit. However, it is possible to leave from other areas of the body, such as the solar plexus or feet. Or one may simply rise out of the physical. The exit is sometimes quite slow and peaceful though it may be abrupt or like an explosion. The body may feel as if it were rocking, or one may have the sensation of being pulled out, as a person would pull something from a tight container. One may also feel tingling and disconnectedness.

It is also possible when astral traveling to look back and see a silver colored cord which attachs the astral body to the physical body. Some persons are fearful that this cord may break prematurely through out-of-body travel and cause death. It is unlikely that this would happen unless it was the person's time to cross over.

Everyone does some astral travel in the sleep state, and the process is the same when awake. The only difference is that you are conscious of it.

Persons also fear that someone may take over their body when they are doing the astral traveling. It is possible that lower level entities may try for entry. This is called "possession." This, too, is rare, since persons developed enough to do astral traveling have developed their bodies to a higher vibration than is usable to lower level entities.

Excess astral traveling does weaken the cord and makes it more difficult to remain in the body. This makes everyday living difficult as a person would be slightly disconnected.

One may pray for protection before traveling and also work toward a more highly refined physical system.

Mental Travel

In mental travel, the consciousness remains in the mental body, although the soul vibrations may go along. The point of exit may be the neck, the back of the head, or the forehead. This type of travel is more subtle and peaceful than astral travel, and the feeling of the body during flight is not there. One usually sees in very sharp detail and color.

It is also possible to travel to places one intends to visit in the future in the physical body. The purpose of such travel is to orient oneself to the area and check out the locations of various points of interest. This can cause a feeling of deja vu, though sometimes such experiences are related to past lives instead.

Sometimes clairvoyance, highly developed, is confused with mental travel. However, clairvoyance is like looking at a flat picture, whereas mental travel has more sense of dimension. Sounds and feelings are not as intense as those experienced during astral travel. The awareness of thought, however, is much stronger. While astral travel is usually limited to our planet, in mental travel the distance increases to include the solar system, and, if highly developed, the galaxy.

Soul Travel

Soul travel is the most recommended and least used of the three forms of out-of-body travel. Much learning and experiencing of dimensions beyond our own can happen this way. One of the most common feelings is that of no longer being a prisoner of this dimension, understanding the freedom we have beyond our known world.

Purposes

Another reason for out-of-body travel is to replenish the system with higher energies. When that is done, the physical body does not have to take in as much energy for the operation of the system, and less food and rest are needed.

A very important reason for studying out-of-body experiences is to understand what they feel like and to know when they happen. The more stress people have in their lives, the more likely they are to unknowingly "separate" their bodies. That is, the astral will separate slightly from the physical so as to reduce the impact of feelings. This is not done consciously, but seems to be an automatic response to protect the system when there is excessive stress. Sometimes a person may use the expression, "I was beside myself." This is not just an expression. It happens. A person with psychic vision looking at that person would see a replica of the actual physical body.

However, this is not a true out-of-body experience, generally speaking. The consciousness stays primarily in the physical body, but, since some of it is in the "extra" body, it is difficult for the person to function normally.

The same may be said for a "mental" split. This is to relieve mental stress rather than emotional and happens in some cases of mental illness.

Soul-level splits or disconnections also occur, especially in times of great guilt, shame, or rejection of the religious or spiritual energies. Those persons who have strong criminal tendencies may have suffered a severe soul-level split. Minor ones happen quite commonly to persons, leaving them with a somewhat "out of sync" feeling.

By practicing basic out-of-body experiences, a person can become aware of such splits and can practice bringing the bodies together again.

It is also possible for one of the bodies to separate, leaving the main consciousness in the physical. A person then has the feeling of not being "all there" or all together. Meditating or focusing on something quite often helps the reintegration of the bodies. A nap also can be helpful, as it allows the bodies some unhampered time to reconnect.

It is useful to be aware of the phenomenon of out-of-body travel, so that if it should happen spontaneously one will be aware of what is happening and get maximum benefit from it.

Conditions

It is very common for persons to travel out of their bodies while sleeping. Traveling in full consciousness, however, is more difficult. Things which help to achieve this are:

- A deep desire to be someplace else.
- A deep desire to see someone else.
- Extreme stress or fear.
- Lack of sleep.

- Alcohol or drugs: This is not recommended procedure as a person's vibrations would be lowered by this practice, leaving the body open for possession by negative entities. Also, one does not have the control needed to return at a certain time, should that be necessary.

- Anesthetic: There are numerous records of persons leaving their bodies under anesthesia and watching an operation performed on their bodies.

- Shock: An impending accident can cause separation which reduces the severity of injuries as the body relaxes.

- Music: Certain kinds of music are conducive to out-of-body experiences. Some music from India and trance-inducing music from other cultures are particularly useful.

How to Know If You Are Really Projecting

There are several indications of true out-of-body travel. One is the feel of wind blowing over you; another is a sense of freedom, lightness, and well being. Some persons look down and see their physical body. You may also see a silvery cord connecting your physical and astral body. Sometimes someone will report that you appeared someplace other than where your physical body actually was. You may awaken with a sense of fear or with noises being loud, out of proportion. Sometimes you can check the experience out by telling someone what you saw when you traveled, if it is something which can be verified. Although things can be seen through clairvoyance also, it is not always an accurate method by itself.

Sometimes the body has a heaviness and you feel yourself slipping away. Some persons think they are dying and try to stay in the body. There usually is a momentary lapse of consciousness in this form of exit from the physical.

Generally, in the higher form of going through the pineal gland or mental areas, there is no lapse of consciousness, and it can happen so quickly that you are out before you know you are going. Some persons just experience floating up into the air.

In mental travel there is little change of consciousness except for the absence of bodily sensations and an awareness of concentrated mental faculties.

In soul-level travel there is no particular body sense as in astral travel, but instead there is a sense of oneness with all.

There is no sensation of barriers with mental or soul travel. In astral travel the wall feels thicker than air, much as water is thicker than air.

Problems

You can awaken in a state of fear or panic from loud noises, or awaken in anger if you were having an "astral argument" with someone. These are not serious problems, but they can leave you quite uncomfortable for awhile.

More troubling may be feeling atmospheric stresses or negativity which you do not understand. You will then awaken with a puzzled, unsettled feeling, which may stay with you awhile.

If astral traveling, you can come back into the body too quickly and too hard, causing a severe pain in the back of the head. This is a crash landing, which usually happens when you are not back before your alarm rings, or there is some other loud noise or some unusual circumstance which pulls you back too quickly. You can avoid this by telling yourself before you travel or before you go to sleep that it is okay to come back quickly but to land gently.

Some people fear possession by discarnate entities during travel. If your body is of higher vibrations this is unlikely. Separation brought about by alcohol or drugs is another story, as that can open you up for possession. As a general rule, fear of possession is unnecessary; however, praying for protection is always a good idea. You may also wish to meditate and put yourself in a higher vibratory level before attempting out-of-body travel.

Some people fear a premature cutting of the silver cord which connects all your bodies. When some bodies leave the physical, this cord can stretch indefinitely. Through it you

maintain your contact with the physical body and its sur-
roundings. If it is your time to go and you are traveling, the
cord will break; otherwise you will return to your body.
However, persons who do excessive conscious out-of-body
traveling may like it so well, they would just as soon not
come back. This may cause a weakness of the cord and eventually lead to premature death. Excessive astral travel can
also bring a loosening of the connection with the physical,
making daily life more difficult to live, and the possibility of
another entity entering your body is more likely.

Some out-of-body travelers visit vibratory levels which
we know as hell or heaven. Some visit other dimensions.
Most of the time there is an understanding of what is going
on but such visits can be frightening or disorienting.

When traveling out of your physical body, please *respect
others' privacy.* Do not intrude where you are not wanted. This
is a misuse of your energy.

What if You Start to Go and Don't Want To?

This is no problem at all. Simply think strongly that you
do not want to go. Your mind is the ultimate controller of
your flights. Stretching the body and moving around will
also hinder leaving.

How Do You Appear?

Oddly enough, you may appear dressed as the physical
body is dressed, or in a different outfit, or completely naked.
Your mind can determine in what you are clothed. In other
words, you can program yourself to appear a certain way.
Sometimes the traveling body just appears naked and you do
not even know it is gone.

A woman in a meditative group was deep in meditation
when another member of the group looked up to see her
floating around the ceiling naked. This is an unusual happening, however. More commonly, your body is not seen at
all, though your presence may be felt.

Meditations for Travel

Some preliminary meditations can be helpful in getting in touch with what it feels like in the astral body, as separate from the physical. The astral body has the general shape of the physical body but can stretch, becoming either elongated or very wide. Parts of the astral body can be quite flexible on their own. Below is an meditation for getting in touch with the astral body.

Meditation — Astral Awareness

Step 1: Lie down, let yourself be totally comfortable, minimize distractions. You may wish to use an astral travel tape or to turn your radio to the white noise (the sound between stations). One of the difficulties with astral tapes is that when the tape ends, the machine clicks off. This can startle the physical body, causing concern in the astral body, which results in a rush-back, unsettling feelings, and perhaps a headache. Lie on your back with your hands by your sides.

Step 2: Have the feeling of floating. Let go.

Step 3: Lift the left astral arm out of the left physical arm. You may need to imagine that this is happening. Energy follows imagination. Imaging or visualizing will eventually bring it out.

Step 4: Let the left astral hand massage your face. Be aware of it.

Step 5: Continue the feeling of floating and let the right astral hand and arm lift out of the physical. Then let your astral hands touch. Let the two astral hands explore each other. You may wish to massage your feet with your astral hands. (The astral body stretches.) Let the astral hands shake hands, part, and then go back into the physical hands and arms.

Step 6: Raise the astral left foot, then the right one. Get the feeling that the astral feet are above the physical ones. If you have to, just imagine it in the beginning; that is alright. Further practice brings greater ability. Let the astral feet sink back into the physical body after a few moments.

Step 7: Let your whole body float, then come back down.

Step 8: Very slowly, now, stretch your legs, arms, and then your whole body. After any deep meditation, you should always stretch to be sure your bodies are all back together; then open your eyes.

Below are several different forms to use for astral projection. You may wish to try each one of them to see which works best for you. Do not wear yourself out trying them all at once. Do be sure to take the time to stretch well after each one, or you may find that you have not reconnected your bodies. You will feel disconnected, spacey, and, perhaps, crabby.

For each of the meditations make sure that you are in a comfortable place with minimal distractions. Be sure there is no tightness in your clothing. The physical body needs to be completely relaxed.

Astral 1

Step 1: Think of someplace you want to go or someone you wish to see, will it, desire it.

Step 2: Transfer consciousness from the physical to the astral body.

Step 3: Imagine separation of your bodies, and then let it happen.

Step 4: In the astral, move around, observe, experiment.

Step 5: Return to your physical body, wait a moment, then stretch.

Astral 2

Step 1: Think of someplace you would like to go.

Step 2: Fill yourself with light lavender with white coming through, medium red, then light blue with a silver and white coming through. Let yourself float.

Step 3: Visualize your astral body inside your physical body, held there by attachments of the chakras (energy vortices). The chakras, when held still and momentarily reversed about an inch, will release the higher bodies. Visualize this happening enough to release the higher bodies.

Step 4: Let yourself go and return in five minutes.

Step 5: When you return, allow the chakras to reconnect and function normally, then take a few minutes to review in your mind where you went and what you saw.

Astral 3

Step 1: Be fully relaxed.

Step 2: Imagine you are pushing the astral form out of your physical. Continue this until you feel a slight tingling. You will feel an emptiness in the physical body. Be at peace with it. Do not pull the astral back. You may feel a coolness in the physical body with the emptiness. Stay at peace. Be aware of any sensations, but do not pay attention to them.

Step 3: Let your consciousness be in the astral. Let it go.

Step 4: Explore and be aware of what you see. As you become more comfortable, experiment with moving around and going places.

Step 5: Return and stretch.

Astral 4

Step 1: Think of the place you want to go. *Really feel* the desire. Will yourself to go.

Step 2: Let yourself get the feeling of floating. Imagine the separation, then transfer consciousness.

Step 3: Return and stretch.

Astral 5

At night before going to sleep, will yourself to go someplace you wish to go, and also will yourself to remember everything you did during your travels, when you awaken.

Many persons have a tendency to live with their astral body slightly disconnected. It is a way of not having to deal with problems or take actions. Also, in cases of severe emotional or physical shock, there may be a separation. Doing the above meditations will help make a person aware that has happened. It can help get the bodies back in touch again.

Mental Travel

In mental travel you do not have the sensations of physical traveling. The awareness is more like observing a scene or watching a movie in your head. A meditation for mental travel is as follows:

Mental 1

Step 1: Where would you like your mental body to go?

Step 2: Put your consciousness in your mental level.

Step 3: Let the mental body leave the physical body.

Step 4: Move around, observe, experiment.

Step 5: Return to your physical body, wait a moment, then stretch.

Mental 2

Choose a planet you feel connected with or which affects your astrological chart heavily. Focus your mental awareness on it. Let your mental consciousness expand, especially from the 5th eye (center of the forehead) and top of your head. Imagine you are seeing that planet. Then let go of the imagination and be aware of thoughts or pictures which come to you.

This may take some practice to achieve, but it is worth the effort. Imagination is a way of focusing energy. Do not hold the imagination longer than a few minutes. Let energy do the rest.

Mental travel can be used to see into the Earth, other places on Earth, the solar system, and into the galaxy.

Do not spend long periods of time with this. It can be tiring and bring headaches if your energies are not sufficiently developed yet.

Soul Travel

Many persons begin the development of their soul-level travel through deep concern or love for others. This deep feeling becomes an energy force to aid in soul travel. It is very common for the persons to be unaware that a part of them — their soul level—has traveled to be with someone else. Sometimes the soul level "body" appears to a person to warn of danger, to comfort, or to encourage. More commonly, the person being "visited" is aware of the visitor's presence rather than actually seeing the body. A traveler who is seen and recognized in one place while his or her physical body is also in another area has experienced bilocation.

There is no restriction as to where our soul-level "body" can travel in the cosmos. Such travel is very difficult for most persons to do in full consciousness, though in more developed persons it happens frequently during dreams.

Soul 1

Before going to sleep, be in a prayerful, loving state. Ask your soul-level body to visit and converse with someone you care about. Ask yourself to remember the visit. Write down what you want to do and then check it in the morning.

This meditation may also be used in astral or mental travel. It is difficult, sometimes, to tell which level went on the journey. As you develop awareness you can tell by the vibrations experienced during the travel which level was used.

Soul 2

Think of some place in the galaxy or universe you would like to go. Concentrate on it for a few minutes, then be in a prayerful state. Concentrate on the top of your head. Think a rush of energy from your heart up and out the top of your head. Be aware. Pictures and awareness will be very subtle at first.

Soul 3

Use the same format as in soul meditation 2, but ask to see your guardian angel or spiritual guides and to converse with them.

CLOSING

There is not much danger of over-separation of bodies when mental- and soul-level travels are practiced. However, too much travel can leave you too spacey. Do not stress your system with traveling or practicing it. You are the best judge of how much is enough.

Be patient with yourself. It can take years to develop good control of this type of travel. It is best to let it rest for periods of time and pick it up again later. This technique allows your system to develop on its own for awhile.

It is a good idea to write down thoughts and impressions you receive in your travels for further study and clarification. There are numerous books on astral travel, and the serious student may wish to do further study on this subject.

Happy traveling!

17

DIMENSIONS AND PLANES—
INNER AND OUTER BODIES

BODIES AND EVOLUTION

We are pure energy—energy with many different frequencies or vibratory rates. In this section we are concentrating on the energy used in our different bodies and how to change the vibratory rates to help in our evolvement.

Our physical body has a heavier, denser form, with lower vibratory rates, the etheric body has a slightly lighter energy form, the emotional body, higher than the etheric and so on. As we purify and refine the energy in our bodies, the bodies change and become what can be called an octave higher. For those of you who are acquainted with music, you know the difference between low "C", middle "C", and high "C". They have the same tone, are very similar to each other, but some have a higher sound and lighter feel, and others have a heavier sound and are lower in pitch. So it is with our bodies. They may change in pitch, but as the tone "C" never becomes a "D", or a "D" never becomes an "E", our physical body never becomes an emotional body, nor does the emotional body ever become a mental body, and so on. Each body retains its basic functions or "tone," but can be so refined and purified as to reach an octave higher.

We keep our bodies separate until very highly developed, when all bodies and functions seem to merge into one source of wisdom, power, and love.

Our seven bodies and their functions are as follows:

- Physical—a living machine for the higher bodies to express through, used for action.

- Etheric (higher form of physical)—connects nerves and higher energies.

- Emotional—a unit for development and use of feelings.

- Mental—a unit for development and use of thought.

- Intuitional/Compassionate—a unit for development and use of understanding and intuition.

- Will/Spirit—a unit for development and use of the will and self.

- Soul—a unit for development and use of the I AM Presence and an awareness of self.

- Divine—a unit for the development and use of divine powers, such as love and healing.

All of these bodies have a capacity to love and be loved, although for some it is not the main function. All bodies also must be fed appropriate "food" for their development, each has the ability to give and receive, and has a power of its own. If one body is developed at the expense of the others, or even one other, at some time that body will lose some of its energy, some of its ability, while the energy goes to help make up the deficit in the deprived body. For instance, a person who drives him or herself mentally may have a mental breakdown, which will give the physical parts a chance to recuperate, if that is where the energy is pulled from. If the emotional energy was drained for mental use, there may be an emotional breakdown. The brain does not want to function as it did before—it does not care what the mind wants to bring through it, it just wants to rest or else has lost ability to function correctly. How many heavily physical persons do you know who function well on higher bodies? Sometime, in this life or another, the other bodies will want equal time.

Each new age brings in stronger energies, which give us an opportunity to cleanse the old bodies and to use the stronger energies to reach a higher octave. This is called purifying and refining. Some persons will use these energies well and quickly, and will develop into the higher octave much faster than the average person. The average person will get there by the end of the particular age, although he or she may not have each body perfected. Slower developing persons will have, of course, much slower development and may be hanging onto their Piscean bodies as their brothers and sisters leave their Aquarian bodies to go into the bodies of the next age.

During the age through which we have just passed, humanity had an octave of bodies which we call the solar person, because the highest energies which the average person was capable of using in his or her system, or being affected by, were those from our solar system. Although higher energies could at times affect the average person, it was uncommon. Highly developed persons could, of course, use much higher energies—such as galactic, universal, or cosmic. The solar system energies consist of those from the Sun, Moon, and planets.

In the Aquarian Age, humanity can now develop into a higher octave which we will call galactic mankind—one who is able to use and be affected by energies from the galaxy. This means planets and suns from other solar systems, plus the galaxy's gravity pull will affect him or her and in turn he or she can learn to use these energies in his or her development. The more highly developed or evolved person will continue to use higher energies but will also be affected by the incoming energies. This ultimately will mean the emergence of a new astrology and much new knowledge.

Another way of describing this is to look at how a radio works. If there isn't any current coming into it, or it isn't turned on, it does little but gather dust. (Have you had days when you just gathered dust?) When the current is on, you can change the frequencies and receive from different stations. If you have a larger radio, then you can bring in more stations and they will be clearer. It is the same with us—we take the energies coming into us and tune into them, and we can feel more, sense more, think more, intuit more, love more, and so on. If we have a larger capacity, we can hear celestial music, voices of spiritual guides, have beautiful spiritual experiences and live more productive, fuller lives. A galactic person is like a larger radio—he or she gets that way by the purifying and refining of his energies, which allows him or her to use higher frequency energies.

THE SEVEN BODIES

The seven bodies relate to the seven planes or dimensions to which our evolution relates. Most person haven't developed very far up the vibratory ladder. In fact, very few persons have developed the physical to its potential.

Evolution calls us to develop abilities in order for us to connect or vibrate with these various levels and develop the abilities to function from them.

Take each body in turn, open the contact point (see chart 6), ask to be in touch with that particular vibratory rate. Be aware of it for a few minutes. Then ask how you are to develop further on that level at this time. If no answer comes, let your mind ramble and feelings surface. This may help you get in touch with the information. Write information down when you get it.

When you have finished the meditation, make plans to work on the information. This will help bring more information in the next time you do the meditation. These bodies relate to the outer world.

Chart 6 CONTACT POINTS FOR BODY LEVELS	
Body	**Contact Point**
Physical	arms and legs
Emotional	navel
Mental	forehead and brain area
Intuitional/Compassionate	heart
Will/Spirit	back and spine
Soul	behind temples, sides of neck as it curves into shoulders, and inside of arms and legs
Divine	top of head

INNER BODIES

We have seven inner bodies that relate to the inner worlds. They are like mirror images of the outer bodies just discussed. Their function is to develop profoundness, inner strength, healing, and strong relationship to earth.

There is negativity and dark forces in the inner world, so always be careful that you recognize both, and protect yourself by flooding any negativity you encounter with white light.

The usual things we see in the inner world are darker forms of colors, black, and silver (like moonlight); occasionally you may see bright colors. However, bright colors and light are usually in the outer bodies.

Depression pushes persons into this area to develop skills mentioned above, but most of the time persons get caught in the "depressing" aspect and don't get the learning.

Shamanism deals beautifully with these levels. Mythology also comes primarily from inner worlds. The primordial force is very strong in the inner worlds.

Meditation to Develop Balance of
Inner and Outer Levels

(Note: For outer bodies your energy needs to flow outward. For inner bodies your energy needs to flow inward.)

You may see animals, mythological animals or persons, or archetypal symbols. You can ask if they have a message for you. If you see something scary, cover it with white light.

In the inner worlds you may see clear colors, muted colors, or velvety black with silver. In the outer worlds, the colors you usually see are vivid and alive.

Make notes of things you wish to remember as you go along. It is difficult to retain memory when you shift levels.

When going into the inner bodies, you may have the feeling of "shifting" dimensions so that you can go deeper.

1. Be aware of the outer physical body (arms and legs) and breathe into it, let it relax (energy going out).
2. Go to the inner physical body (energy going in).
3. Feel a balance between outer and inner bodies.
4. Fill the space between the outer and inner bodies with love, clarity, and blessing.

Continue the meditation, doing the same for the other six levels. (You will note that the distance between the bodies increases at each level). On the seventh levels, focus your attention on God "beyond" the body and God "within" the body.

Color Meditation

Fill yourself with the contemplative (high spiritual) color, then the action color (bright shades), and then with the darker color which will bring the energy into the inner levels. It may feel as though the darker color "thuds" into your body, but that is all right. It feels like it is lower, but that is just because it goes into inner levels.

Thirty seconds per shade of color is enough in the beginning. You may wish to work up to longer periods of time, such as five minutes per shade, as information quite often comes in from the various vibrations reached through the colors.

See Color Chart for Inner and Outer Levels (chart 7).

SAMADHI AND BODY LEVELS

Samadhi is a Sanskrit word that means balanced or even. When a person reaches this state of balance or evenness it opens the door to greater spiritual states. There are several levels of samadhi and various ways in which to work with it. Below is a meditation using one form of samadhi:

Tune into the inner divine level, then balance that with the outer Divine level. Feel balance or evenness between these two areas. Breathe into the vibration of the evenness. Slowly let the energy of the evenness expand as far out and around your body as you can without losing the sense of evenness. Then hold it there and breathe into it peacefully and deeply. Observe what happens with your system. Several minutes is long enough in the beginning, gradually working your way up to ten minutes. This is a very powerful meditation and you may find it releases a lot of energy. It helps to speed development.

Chart 7
COLOR CHART FOR INNER AND OUTER LEVELS

Contemplative	Action	Inner World	Function
Light Pink	Bright Pink	Dark Pink	Creativity, focusing change energy
Light Rose	Bright Rose	Dark Rose	Love and connectiveness
Light Melon	Bright Orange	Dark Orange	Power and intensity
Light Yellow	Bright Yellow	Dark Yellow	Mental
Light Green	Bright Green	Forest Green	Healing, growth, relationships
Light Blue	Bright Blue	Midnight Blue	Devotion, ideals
Lavender	Bright Purple	Indigo	Wholeness, expansion
White Light	Radiant Light	Iridescent Gray-White, pearly	Spiritual

18

GUIDES, ANGELS, AND OTHER ENTITIES

CLOSE ENCOUNTERS

Most persons will, sometime in their meditative practice, become aware of other entities. This is normal. Mediation opens you to other areas which may be called levels, planes, dreams, or alternate realities. These areas are occupied by other beings.

Sometimes a deceased relative or friend may appear, or an angelic presence. Sometimes higher-level beings will appear who act as spiritual guides. These usually are very blessed events.

Not so blessed an event is when negative images appear, such as persons with horrible grimaces on their faces, or entities which seem negative or evil. If this happens, filling and surrounding yourself in a radiant light can help dispel them. Calling on God, Jesus, or whomever you relate to as a spiritual being, to help remove them works.

You may also call on the "spiritual bouncers" to take the person or persons back to where they need to be. I use the term "spiritual bouncers" to refer to those persons in the planes of afterlife whose mission it is to help guide persons to where they need to be. They don't mind the use of the term.

The negative, or evil, entities appear for several reasons:

- In your meditation you may have reached an area where they exist.

- There may be negativity around you which attracts them.

- It may be time in your growth to learn to handle this type of energy. It is one of the energy tests we all go through.

- You may have been involved in negativity in past lives.

No matter the reason for the intrusion, you must learn to dispel them. The suggestions listed above usually do the trick.

If you see a deceased person or friend, they usually just want to say "hello" and let you know they still live, even if the body doesn't. Sometimes they have messages, quite often of encouragement. If you have trouble hearing them, let your mind be open. They can then "imprint" on your thought process and you can receive the message. You are not bound to follow any suggestions if you don't wish to, or if they don't seem to be in your best interests. One shouldn't use relatives and friends as "guides," as it puts too much strain on them in their development, and their judgment may be no better than yours. Remember, you are ultimately responsible for all you do, no matter where the advice comes from!

The veils between this plane and the after-death planes are becoming thinner, and the visiting is becoming easier. This method can be used sometimes to heal hurt feelings or misunderstandings which arose in the Earth plane.

GUIDES

There are many levels of persons—entities—from other planes who serve as guides for particular projects of a person's life.

Some are lower level ones who don't know that much, but like to control or meddle. Their information is usually incorrect and they are quite often "bossy" to the point of wanting to take over another person's life. It is best not to become involved with them.

Lower level guides quite often wear a person out, causing them to be subject to much illness or discomfort.

Sometimes persons who have achieved much in the same area will work with persons who have similar interests and vibrations, to help continue the work they started.

Everyone has a guardian angel who is with them all of the time. Their ability to work with us is strengthened and becomes more effective as we open to them. If a person is doing something that has great ramifications for the development of civilization, there will be many angels and guides to help in the overall program.

Persons upon death do not become angels. They are on a different evolutionary track. Persons can and do become "as" angels, however, but retain their own functions.

Angels will work primarily with a person's soul and spiritual development and the higher, more spiritual guides (persons who become "as" angels) will work more with the evolutionary development of the planet through a person or persons who agree to do this work. These beings do not try to take over your life and are very careful for the well-being of the person and his or her body.

Higher level guides are persons who have lived on the Earth plane and achieved great growth and expertise in some area. They then work with others on Earth who are involved in a similar area.

Contact directly with the God force brings a person in contact with the full spectrum of information and energy. Angels and higher guides are directed from this force.

However, we are all equally important in the eyes of God as each person has his or her own tasks. Some are accomplished on earth and some in other dimensions. All are important in the scheme of things.

It's not that one's work is more important than another's. It's how well you do what is yours to do.

Failing

Persons sometimes fall short of their own glory for any number of reasons. Some are:

- Fear of handling stronger energies, greater tasks.

- Fear of change.

- They may have turned the energy to their own private use.

- Ego wants to direct and a person loses contact with the God force.

- The "why me" syndrome—one may feel inadequate.

Working with Guides

How is a person chosen to become a partner in evolutionary work? This work may include healing, helping others in distress, bringing in a new world order, or bringing in new teachings. Many times persons will have made a commitment to do these things before being born.

When a person has achieved a certain amount of light vibration he or she will begin to resonate with higher purpose. They will then be watched by higher guides and some guidance given. As the person develops more of the light vibration and more trust in the evolutionary process, they will be given more work to do. We become hands and feet for God and the higher beings. Our minds become vessels for new information and our hearts become vessels for love and compassion.

The person will then dedicate more and more of his or her life to the project, sometimes achieving superhuman levels. Cooperation between earth plane beings and higher guides and angels is incredible in terms of what can be accomplished. The higher guides and angels always work within the framework of God's Divine Plan.

How to Open to Contact

Many times persons will feel they are on the edge of receiving information and guidance and can't quite make the connection. It takes time to prepare oneself to hear and see on these higher, more subtle levels. A person may have the vibrational potential but just hasn't learned to make it workable.

Following are some requirements:

- Taking quiet time so as to tune into the higher vibrations.

- Willingness and ability to let your ego open up (not shut down, as that can lead to possession or discordance) to see or hear information.

- Willingness to take the time for these extra projects. They usually come *in addition* to what you are already doing. Later you may be able to do them full time.

- A groundedness with God and Earth so that you can comprehend the bigger plans.

- Absence of prejudice, because this can affect what you receive.

- The person's brain will need to be flexible and be developed so that comprehension of new ideas is possible. Rigid attitudes and egotism block this type of contact.

- A belief in the greater good of mankind and the evolutionary process.

- Faith even though in doubt.

Developing Contact with Guides and Angels

The voices of guides and angels are usually very subtle and are similar to intuitions. It is as though they implant a thought form into a psychic sounding board in the head, and then it manifests in our language. The higher, more spiritual guides or angels are not interested in telling you every little thing to do. They do not want to interfere with your karma and your growth. They are, however, ready and willing to help, when you are ready and willing to grow and expand, and they are especially helpful when you are working in an area of service. They work with the overall plan of evolution, and work through natural processes. They can and do, however, create or help create miracles at times. They do not take away your personal responsibilities in life, unlike lower level guides who like to control and dictate what you do.

A gentleman told me he wanted to be in contact with his guides, but he wanted someone to appear in front of him and speak out loud. Certainly this would make it easier for us. But very seldom does it ever happen that way.

There are a number of ways which can help us to open to this contact. Usually through our spiritual development we develop the contact and awareness of it. Sometimes persons say a message "came out of the blue," and for many that is the way they receive the message.

Methods of contact include:

- Conversation

- Synchronicity or blending of energies

- Thoughts or ideas impressed on a person's mind

- Feelings imparted to a person

- Intuitions

- Information received through others

- Information received through reading

MEDITATIONS—GETTING IN TOUCH

Devotional Chakra

Opening the devotional chakra in the center of the back of the head sometimes facilitates hearing the voices of the higher spiritual guides. The messages are usually very subtle or quiet, and you need to be relaxed and aware in order to hear them.

Meditation

Feel your devotional chakra as open, be relaxed and aware, and ask to remember a time when you did understand a message from them, even if you didn't know its source. Ask what messages a guide or angel has been trying to get through to you recently. Ask your guide or angel what question you should be asking, then ask that question. Let your mind be open. It may come in very clearly or you may have to let your mind ramble in order for it to form a thought or it may come in as an insight or intuition several days later.

6th Level Contact

Ask to be in touch with your 6th level brain vibration. Be into it; breathe into it. Let your consciousness develop in it. Ask to feel the presence of the spiritual guides or angels. Ask to feel by osmosis (by absorption) any messages or information they may have for you.

OTHER INFORMATION SOURCES

Consciousness

All energies have consciousness, and if a person learns to tune into the vibrations, much information can come.

Inner World

Sometimes power animals and mythological beings give guidance from the inner worlds.

Universal Stream of Consciousness

This is a vibration that contains all information that has been known, is known, and will be known.

Prayer

Prayer is, for many, the best source of guidance. The greater the person's prayer life, the richer are it's rewards. Contact with God through prayer can activate all channels of information.

Persons sometimes look for a magic source that will answer all questions and make all decisions. If that were possible, it would take away our opportunities for growth and development. It is great to receive knowledge and guidance, but no matter the source of the information, we are still responsible for how we use it or don't use it. It is up to us to make the final decisions in our life.

19

CONTEMPLATIVE STATE

A person who has developed beyond the meditative state lives in, and expresses, the contemplative state. Even if a person is not yet at that level, it is good to practice some of the abilities as a way of opening quicker to these vibrations— a taste of what is to come.

Some of the attributes of the contemplative person (with meditations) are listed below:

1. In the contemplative state it is possible to experience *oneness.*

Sometimes the oneness of something nearby, but totally unrelated, will occur. I had read a number of accounts of great oneness with the universe occurring, or other uplifting happenings. My first oneness was with a chest of drawers next to where I was lying. It wasn't very uplifting, but I did experience the total oneness with it. The next time this happened was with a bug on the window I was lying near. This certainly was more interesting, as it was a more active life form. Still it was rather humbling—what happened to oneness with God and the Universe? Eventually, I did experience that. I still treasure the oneness with the chest of drawers and the bug. The objects may not have been that high on the evolutionary scale, but the oneness was great, and life where they are has its own meaning.

Meditation A

Choose a flower, tree, spiritual personage, universe, or God. Concentrate on your choice, then be open to receiving energy (the meditative state). After a few minutes of this, expand and open to become one with your choice.

It may take time for you to truly feel the deep oneness, but each time you open to it you get closer.

Meditation B

Lying or sitting comfortably, breathe deeply and extend your consciousness in order to fill the entire cosmos. Be one with it. Be aware of what your consciousness comprehends. When fully developed, this brings consciousness of the cosmos or "cosmic consciousness."

Meditation C

The opposite of the above meditation is to become one with the smallest unit that we know—currently it is the quark. Let your consciousness go deep inside something and find a quark. Become one with it.

The contemplative is aware of the great and the small.

2. The contemplative recognizes that what is here of "you" is only an extension of the greater self—*the soul.*

Meditation A

Ask to feel yourself as a manifestation of your soul's thought form. Feel the greater consciousness of your soul-level. Be one with your soul-level.

Meditation B

Be one with the heaven levels (7th heaven if you choose). Feel the greater life that exists there. Be one with the greater energy—the eternal life force.

3. The contemplative is *filled with light*. The person's vibrations are so high that they radiate.

Meditation A

Be aware of the superficial fascia just under your skin, all over your body. Feel that area as light, and filled with very refined vibrations. Have the feeling of floating, and let the light and refined vibrations permeate your entire body and radiate from you.

Meditation B

Do the same as above, but also bring light from the inner 7th level to match the outer 7th level light.

Meditation C

Imagine a developed aura around you. Fill it with all the tertiary colors (refer to chart 7), beginning with rosy-gold next to your body. The next layer is gold, followed by yellow-green, aqua, lilac, and red-violet. Complete with radiant white around it. Be sure the colors are iridescent in quality. They will feel vibrant and alive. This helps to center and raise your vibrations.

If you feel crabby or restless afterward, take it easy on this meditation until later, when you have adjusted to the force of these energies better.

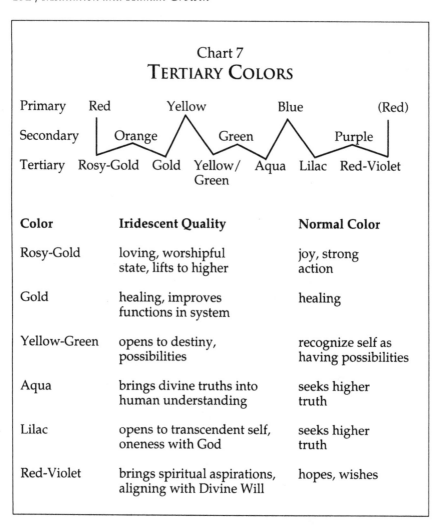

Chart 7
TERTIARY COLORS

Primary	Red		Yellow		Blue		(Red)
Secondary		Orange		Green		Purple	
Tertiary	Rosy-Gold	Gold	Yellow/ Green	Aqua	Lilac	Red-Violet	

Color	Iridescent Quality	Normal Color
Rosy-Gold	loving, worshipful state, lifts to higher	joy, strong action
Gold	healing, improves functions in system	healing
Yellow-Green	opens to destiny, possibilities	recognize self as having possibilities
Aqua	brings divine truths into human understanding	seeks higher truth
Lilac	opens to transcendent self, oneness with God	seeks higher truth
Red-Violet	brings spiritual aspirations, aligning with Divine Will	hopes, wishes

4. **A contemplative is *aware of time and space* as non-fixed vibrations and is able to work with them.**

Meditation A

Breathe peacefully and deeply, with emphasis on the chest. Expand the sides. As you breathe the sides, then open front and back. Ask to feel the vibration of time in your chest, and then in your body.

Get the feeling of slowing time down, allowing you to get into the fullness of it. Ask what have you not been taking time to experience?

Meditation B

Do the same as above, only fill yourself with space. Get the feeling of having plenty of space inside, even if you live and work in crowded spaces.

Meditation C

Feel yourself as lifted up beyond the time prism to where all time is one.

Meditation D

Raise your vibrations up above the space prism and feel all space as one.

5. **The contemplative *is no longer mystified* by the mysteries, but understands them. The contemplative also understands the workings of miracles, and feels continual oneness with God.**

Meditation A

Feel yourself as a part of God. Let that part be in oneness with the totality of God.

Meditation B

Think of a miracle that intrigues you. Feel it in your body. Be one with it. Does it reveal its mysteries to you?

6. One of the most important meditations to help in developing the vibrations of a contemplative is that of *just being.*

Meditation A

Put yourself in a comfortable position with a minimum of distractions. Just be. Don't be thinking or doing or experiencing. Just be.

Meditation B

Try to do the same when you are around distractions.

It takes a long time to develop to the state of being contemplative. However, anything you can do toward even tasting it will enhance your entire growth.

20

CLOSING

E volution pushes us continually onward. If we go with it, work with it, open to it, life, although still a challenge, can be very interesting and rewarding. If we push against it or try to stop its forward movement, the challenges turn to struggles.

Meditation is one way in which we can open to the greater picture of where we are called to be. It is also a viable way of working with it.

Whether to have a meditation practice or not really isn't a valid question anymore. Rather the question should be, "How can I develop the best meditation program for me?"

As you advance, you will feel a stronger need to develop meditation styles and practices which are more conducive to your growth, so try out different combinations of what you already know or do, as well as designing completely new forms.

Do not do the same type of meditations over and over. You will have a tendency to put your vibrations into a rut and then to dig an even deeper hole. Persons who stay with one style of meditation excessively can be just as rigid in their thinking and living as persons who never meditate.

The use of this book and others can give you ideas and directions. Ultimately, however, you are the "book" you will need to read.

Your own "I AMNESS," as connected to your creator, is the greatest source book you will ever have. Let the meditation practice you decide upon enhance the development of the inner you.

May all your meditations be what they need to be.

BIBLIOGRAPHY

Assagioli, Roberto, M.D. *Psychosynthesis.* New York: Penguin, 1971.

The Holy Bible, English translation.

Irion, J. Everett. *Interpreting the Revelation with Edgar Cayce.* Virginia Beach, VA: ARE Press, 1982.

Leadbeater, C. W. *The Inner Life*, Vols I & II, and other publications. Wheaton, IL: Theosophy Society Publishing House, 1978.

Maclean, Dr. Paul D. *The Triune Brain in Evolution: Role in Paleocerebral Functions.* New York: Plenum Publishing, 1989.

Paulson, Genevieve Lewis. *Kundalini and the Chakras.* St. Paul: Llewellyn Publications, 1991.

Ramacharka, Yogi. *Science of Breath.* Homewood, IL: Yoga Publishing Society.

INDEX

Chakra Healing and Karmic Awareness

KEITH SHERWOOD

Accumulating karmic baggage—the dense energy carried from one lifetime to another—is a common hazard for many. This debilitating energy can negatively influence one's personality, relationships, physical health, and spirituality.

The author of *Chakra Therapy* offers a step-by-step approach to overcoming karmic baggage and energy blockages. Keith Sherwood's easy techniques can help you activate the chakras, strengthen boundaries (the surface of auras), arouse the kundalini, and embrace personal dharma. He also teaches how to take care of your energy system and condition it for physical, mental, emotional, and spiritual wellbeing.

0-7387-0354-0
312 pp., 6 x 9, illus. $14.95

To order, call 1-800-THE MOON
Prices subject to change without notice

Kundalini and the Chakras
A Practical Manual—Evolution in this Lifetime

GENEVIEVE PAULSON

The mysteries of Kundalini revealed! We all possess the powerful evolutionary force of Kundalini that can open us to genius states, psychic powers, and cosmic consciousness. More people are experiencing the "big release" spontaneously but have been ill-equipped to channel its force in a productive manner. This book shows you how to release Kundalini gradually and safely, and is your guide to sating the strange, new appetites which result when life-in-process "blows open" your body's many energy centers.

The section on chakras brings new understanding to these "dials" on our life machine (body). It is the most comprehensive information available for cleansing and developing the chakras and their energies. Read *Kundalini and the Chakras* and prepare to make a quantum leap in your spiritual growth!

0-87542-592-5

224 pp., 6 x 9, illus., 6-page color insert $14.95

New Chakra Healing

The Revolutionary 32-Center Energy System

CYNDI DALE

Break through the barriers that keep you from your true purpose with *New Chakra Healing*. This manual presents never-before-published information that makes a quantum leap in the current knowledge of the human energy centers, fields, and principles that govern the connection between the physical and spiritual realms.

By working with your full energy body, you can heal all resistance to living a successful life. The traditional seven-chakra system was just the beginning of our understanding of the holistic human. Now Cyndi Dale's research uncovers a total of 32 energy centers: 12 physically oriented chakras, and 20 energy points that exist in the spiritual plane. She also discusses auras, rays, kundalini, mana energy, karma, dharma, and cords (energetic connections between people that serve as relationship contracts). In addition, she extends chakra work to include the back of the body as well as the front, with detailed explanations on how these energy systems tie into the spine. Each chapter takes the reader on a journey through the various systems, incorporating personal experiences, practical exercises, and guided meditation.

1-56718-200-3

304 pp., 7 x 10, illus., 4-color insert $17.95

To order, call 1-800-THE MOON

Prices subject to change without notice